JOHN POWLESS

A LIFE WELL PLAYED

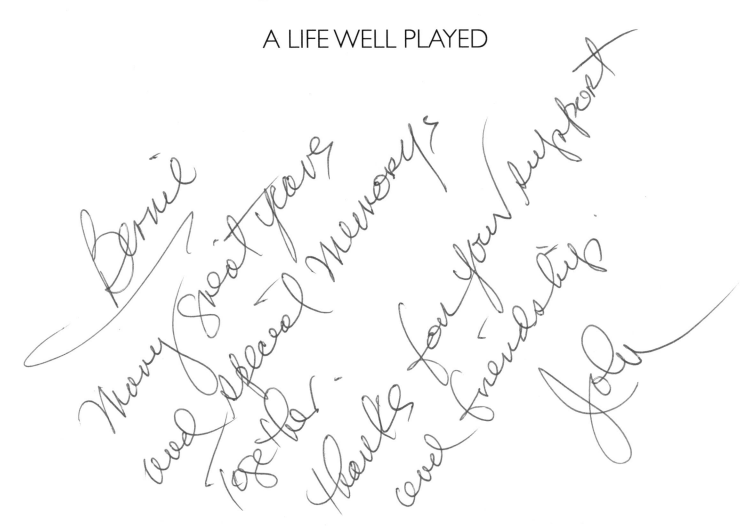

Bernie
Many great years
and special memories
together —
Thanks for your support
and friendship
John

Triangle Media Works, LLC
6922 Winstone Drive
Madison, WI 53711

First Triangle Media Works, LLC publishing edition: 2016

For information about special discounts for bulk purchases or to arrange an appearance by the author or John Powless at a live event contact Triangle Media Works, LLC at 608-271-2964 or visit our web sites at trianglemediaworks.com or johnpowless.com.

Photography and image credits are on page 128.

ISBN: 978-0-9971794-0-8

FOR OUR FAMILIES

CONTENTS

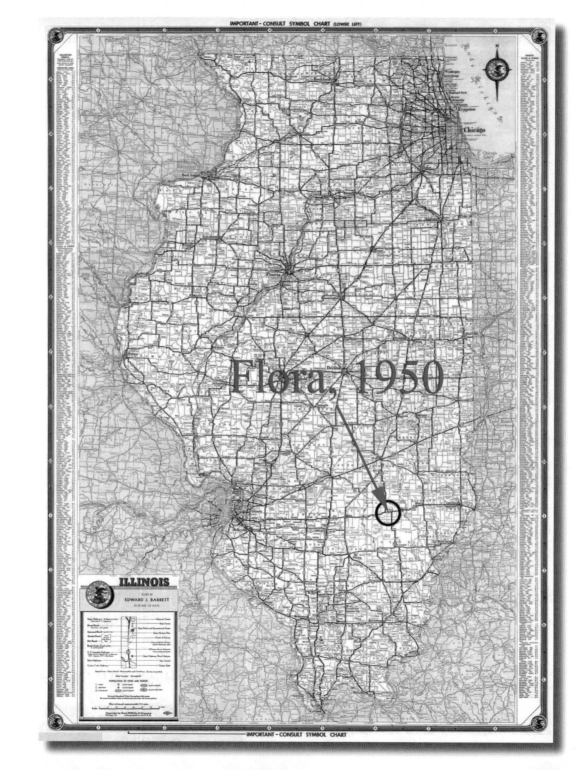

Flora, 1950

PREFACE

John Powless and I met when I was a local television host at WMTV in Madison, Wisconsin. The program at the time featured a different location every night and this particular night we hosted the show from the John Powless Tennis Center in Madison. I must admit I didn't know a lot about John at the time. Little did I know I would come to know a lot about John over the next few years.

We worked together in 1992 producing telecasts for the University of Wisconsin basketball team. John, a former coach of the Badgers, did the color commentary and I produced. Our routine for away games was to fly a small plane from Madison to the away game, produce the show and fly back to Madison where we would end the evening at Babe's Grill and Bar, just up the street from the tennis center.

One game took us to Bloomington, Indiana, where the Badgers were crushed by the Hoosiers. After the game, the play-by-play guy, Mike Heller, and I were anxious to get the hell out of Bloomington. John Powless, however, was in a deep conversation with a man and a young kid. The conversation went on and on as did our fear that we would miss last call at Babe's back in Madison. When John finally ended his conversation and joined us I had to ask who he was talking to: An ex-player, coach, family member?

"John, who were you talking to?"

"I have no idea," replied John.

That's pretty much all you need to know about John Powless but there is a lot more.

This book is a result of conversations with John over a five-year period. Not included is every story he shared with me over our more than 25 year relationship.

Here, he talks about his days on the prairie, rising through the ranks of competitive tennis, coaching the likes of Arthur Ashe, playing and coaching basketball, traveling the world playing with presidents, princes, emperors, movie stars and just hitting a tennis ball against a wall.

He may have won more world titles than the New York Yankees but he still has time for some guy he's never met in Bloomington, Indiana.

Dan Smith
Madison, Wisconsin

Chapter 1

THE PRAIRIE

John Powless grew up somewhere between the movies *It's A Wonderful Life,* the 1946 film in which a young George Bailey worked in a small-town pharmacy, and *Hoosiers,* the 1986 film set in a small-town basketball gym.

He's modest about his successes: his All-American college tennis career; his two NCAA basketball national championship rings; his 36 (and counting) world tennis championships; his careers as player, coach, and broadcaster. The Professional Tennis Registry recently named him the Senior Player of the Millennium (for the 20th century) during a ceremony at the Germantown Cricket Club in Philadelphia.

From the Frog Island Tennis Club in Flora, Illinois, to the grass courts of the Queensland Tennis Centre in Brisbane, Australia, John Powless has played tennis on virtually every tennis surface in the world—including those belonging to the emperor of Japan and the White House. Yet, with all those accomplishments stacked one on top of the other like Lego blocks, Powless, now in his 80s, was—and still is—never in it for the glory. He's just got game, and he's probably most comfortable hitting a tennis ball against any wall available or with his son, Jason, and members of the John Powless Tennis Center in Madison, Wisconsin. And despite four knee surgeries and numerous operations to fix injuries, he still trains every day he's able—for the next tournament in the next city in the next country.

On a recent trip to Turkey, Powless contracted a virus that

sent him to the local hospital. Before he was admitted, he called a longtime friend, plastic surgeon Dr. Steve Bernsten.

"Whatever you do, don't let them use any needles on you," advised Bernsten, who knows a thing or two about the importance of sterile medical instruments.

When the doctor came in wielding needles for an injection, Powless asked for his clothes, grabbed a taxi to the airport, flew to Austria, and checked himself into a hospital he knew would be safe.

"You learn where to go and where not to go," he says. Soon he was back to international competition.

John Dale Powless grew up in Flora, a small town in southern Illinois. Today, Interstates 64 and 57 allow travelers to bypass Flora. But in John Powless' day, Flora was an American crossroads: the junction of U.S. 50 running

John Powlesss was born on August 24, 1932

east and west and U.S. 45 running north and south. If you were headed to St. Louis from Baltimore, you drove through downtown Flora—right past the drugstore where Powless earned a nickel an hour making ham and cheese sandwiches for the men who worked at the Baltimore and Ohio Railroad and roundhouse.

Flora is in the middle of southern Illinois, about a hundred miles east of St. Louis, Missouri. Topographically, it is flat as a table. Prairie grasses could reach as high as a horse, or so Powless' great-grandfather claimed. Flora was built to attract the railroads, which it did, and by the 1930s you worked either for the railroad, on a farm or for a small manufacturing company. In 1934, oil was discovered near Flora and Flora became the center of the businesses it generated.

Powless' parents, Cecil James and Mildred Marie Parish Powless, were also born and raised near Flora. Mildred gave birth to John on August 24, 1932. John was the oldest of three children. His sister, Kay, followed, and brother Bob came along three years later.

On the day John Powless was born, Franklin Roosevelt was three months away from defeating President Herbert Hoover. Amelia Earhart had recently completed the first solo flight by a woman across the Atlantic. *"Brother, Can You Spare a Dime?"* became one of the most popular songs of the year. One of the great tennis players of any era, H. Ellsworth (Elly) Vines, won both the Wimbledon and the United States Lawn Tennis Association singles titles.

John Powless was born into a world where the economy was in the midst of a spectacular, historic free fall. More than 11 million Americans were unemployed. Those who kept their jobs watched their salaries decrease by 40 percent. Wages were 60 percent less than they were in 1929. Farmers watched nervously as production outstripped demand and banks foreclosed on the farms around them. Farmers had been generally hurting since 1920, and by 1932 it became clear that no relief was in sight.

Mildred's father had a farm roughly two and half miles outside of Flora, and it was just hanging on. They grew a variety of crops and kept a few cows to meet the needs of the family. There was no running water or electricity—these amenities were just beginning to find their way to rural areas—and nothing was motorized. Every able family member worked on the farm. As soon

Top: John, Mildred, Bob and Kay about 1941.
Bottom: John on the horse "Rowdy" with a few cousins.

as John was old enough to carry a hoe or walk a horse, Mildred and Cecil sent John to work for his grandfather.

John remembers doing all the chores at one time or another under the eye of Grandpa Parish: sweeping the barn, plowing the fields, and splitting wood to keep the potbellied stove burning in the kitchen. "It lengthened my arms," he chuckles.

He was also in charge of keeping the animals in the barn. "Hans, the riding horse, is out. Go get him," great-grandfather Fabler would tell John through the kitchen window. John never knew why his great-grandfather called him Hans. It never occurred to John to ask.

One of John's duties was to ride the old plug horse bareback into town for supplies. If it was a Saturday, he tied it up outside the movie theater while he went inside to watch the matinee. Riding home alone across the prairie he imagined

A Powless family reunion from about 1940.
That's John front row, right.

himself as the star of one of the matinees—Gene Autry, Sunset Carson or Hopalong Cassidy—saving the frail Mary Meeker from impending doom.

"I thought I could trust you, kid," young John would tell an imaginary bad guy. John says these cinematic escapes helped him forget just how hard he worked on the farm.

When he stayed on the farm, a day in the life meant waking up early in the morning for chores, then off to school, followed by football, basketball or tennis practice, whichever was in season. After practice, it was back to the farm to finish his evening chores, do his homework and get back home in time for bed by nine o'clock. Not that all this was his choice. It's what you did if your family owned a farm.

And it was the farm that insulated the family from the effects of the Depression.

"We didn't have anything invested in the stock market. We were hardworking farm people. Life didn't change very much for us at all," remembers the young farmhand.

Chapter 2

THE SODA JERK

In 1909 a pharmacist named John H. Throgmorton moved to Flora, bought the Eagle Drugstore and renamed it the Throgmorton Drugstore. Mr. Throgmorton never married or had children, yet he would become known as "the father of Flora tennis." His enthusiasm for sports, particularly tennis, spread among the young people of Flora. His drugstore became the local place to talk about the sports scene of the day and to organize unofficial tennis tournaments in the community. He formed the Flora Tennis Team, which played intercity matches against other southern Illinois towns like Salem, Effingham and Mt. Vernon. From 1909 until 1932, the Flora Tennis Team never lost a match.

In 1925, Mr. Throgmorton hired high school freshman Cecil Powless to work in his store. Apparently, Mr. Throgmorton first noticed the nine-year-old Cecil hustling newspapers on the train. Cecil would pick up his newspapers from the drugstore, hop on the train and sell them to the passengers. The papers usually sold out before the train stopped eight miles down the track, where Cecil would hop off and use his charm, his thumb and sometimes his feet to get back to town. Evidently, Mr. Throgmorton liked the kid's work ethic. Little did he know Cecil Powless would one day become his business partner.

Mr. Throgmorton became not only his boss but also a father figure to Cecil. Cecil scooped ice cream, made sandwiches, swept the floor, delivered medicines and did whatever else Mr. Throgmorton asked of his young soda jerk. Cecil also studied pharmacy on the job from Mr. Throgmorton and passed his Illinois pharmacy licensing tests without going to school— one of the last licensed pharmacists in the state of Illinois to do so. Mr. Throgmorton liked Cecil's commitment to the pharmacy profession and in 1947 made him a partner in the business without any financial investment. He renamed the business the Throgmorton-Powless Drugstore.

After several years of farmwork, John Powless followed his father to the drugstore, where he too did everything he was asked to do. Now instead of doing the farm chores, he went directly to the drugstore to work before school. At noon he would sprint back to the store to make sandwiches for the lunch crowd that included many of his classmates. After lunch he sprinted back to school for classes and sports team practices, then back to the drugstore for closing chores, then home for homework and bed by nine. The city may have replaced the farm, but Cecil made sure nothing replaced the work ethic.

John can still describe most details of the store. It was long and narrow. When you entered from Main Street there were two large glass display cases decorated with crepe paper commemorating a holiday or announcing a sale. He remembers the "official" Western Union time clock. The only other official time clock hung at the railroad station. A Western Union employee came in regularly to open the clock with a key to make sure everything worked. Below the clock sat the magazine rack filled with titles like *Look*, *Life* and *The Saturday Evening Post*. On the lower level of the magazine rack were the most important magazines to the kids of Flora: comic books.

"Mr. Throgmorton would let every kid in town come in and read them. I don't think he ever sold one," says John.

The kids would sit on the floor for hours reading the *Adventures of Superman*, *Al Capp's Adventures of Shoo*, *Popeye and the Sky Blazers*.

Cecil "Kayo" Powless

"Mr. Throgmorton reasoned that kids had plenty of places to get into trouble, but no one ever got in trouble sitting on the floor reading *Captain America*," says John.

John remembers the other staples of a drugstore on Main Street: Copenhagen, Shoal and Redman tobacco, Lucky Strike cigarettes. The peanut machine rotated pecans, cashews and other nuts. Bay Rum was the aftershave of choice.

"Guys who were cut off from the bars would buy gallons of Bay Rum to substitute for the booze they couldn't buy," John remembers.

John, as his father before him had, worked the soda fountain, a staple in any drug store of the period. Two ice cream tables seated four each. Down the aisle from the tables were four booths, but only Mr. Throgmorton was allowed in the back booth.

In the back of the store Cecil would mix the various medications used in the pharmacy. John remembers wrapping Evening of Paris perfume and Whitman Samplers chocolates, especially at Christmastime. One of the perks of the job was an unlimited supply of milkshakes.

"I tried every conceivable flavor," remembers John. "The worst was tomato. I tried to pour it out after the first sip, but Mr. Throgmorton had a strict rule that if you made it, you drank it, and sure enough, he was staring right at me. I was sure I would be sick."

Every Saturday night, farmers brought their families dressed in their best clothes to the drugstore and treated them to milkshakes. John knew everybody by name and, of course, their favorite flavors.

One of the busiest times of day was the railroad shift change around seven in the morning. In the back door came the night shift workers for a signature meal of pressed ham and cheese sandwiches and milkshakes. Those on their way into work came in the front door, picked up their tobacco supplies and left through the back.

John and younger brother, Bob

One particularly dapper gentleman came in one day inquiring about the store's milkshake reputation. John says Clark Gable savored every drop.

John Throgmorton with John and Cecil Powless. The Powless men both worked for Mr. Throgmorton and Cecil would eventually become part owner of the pharmacy.

Chapter 3

COACH DANCEY

Thanks to the efforts of Mr. Throgmorton and other sports enthusiasts, athletics became a big part of life in Flora. Another man who got the balls rolling was Bert Dancey. In 1927, this University of Illinois graduate accepted his first teaching and coaching job in Flora. Dancey had played on the same college football team as the legendary Red "Galloping Ghost" Grange, likely the best all-around athlete in America. Dancey would go on to coach football at Flora High School for 31 years. He won 10 North Egypt Conference titles and coached three undefeated teams.

Coach Dancey believed sports discipline was essential for young men, and he managed to convince the mothers and fathers of Flora that his sports regimen was good for the community, too. Sports were not an end but a means for developing discipline and leadership. Most everyone bought into Dancey's plan.

Immediately after the last second ticked off the clock of the last football game of the season, basketball hoops appeared all over town, and all the young men of Flora dutifully reported for basketball practice the very next day. When the buzzer sounded in the last basketball game of the season, the hoops disappeared and the tennis court nets went up. This regimen and seasonal cycle of practice and competition repeated for the entire 31 years of Bert Dancey's coaching tenure.

Every male student at every grade level knew the Danc-

ey plays by heart. You learned your first plays in grade school. One week during recess you'd learn one play. The next week you'd run another play but in a different position. As each of the boys grew in both years and size he played and learned every position. By the time a young man reached high school he knew every play and could run them from every position.

Coach Dancey kept it simple. There were six plays, numbered sequentially. Coach Dancey never varied the playbook, and to this day John can still diagram the plays on the back of an envelope.

John learned basketball

from his neighbor, Skip Hogan. Skip shot left-handed, so John shot left-handed even though he did everything else right-handed. His ambidexterity would serve him well throughout his athletic pursuits.

"It worked to my advantage," John told a sportswriter years later. "It helped my basketball. At least my other hand wasn't so foreign."

Once while John was pitching a softball game left-handed, the other team laid a bunt down the third baseline, betting that the lefty on the mound could not make the throw to first. John foiled the plan when he picked up the ball and threw the runner out at first—right-handed.

John was six feet tall and weighed 115 pounds when he entered Flora High School. His ability to use either hand served him well as a basketball player.

John broke into the starting lineup in his junior year: quite an accomplishment in the Coach Dancey system. He became known as a good shooter with good defensive skills. By his senior year he measured six-foot-five, but at 185 pounds he was still considered skinny. The Flora team was the tallest team in Illinois and one of the most successful.

In football, John played end on both offense and defense. And while Coach Dancey spoke softly, he had a bag full of mental and physical motivational techniques.

Coach Dancey taught his linemen the same three-point stance position they used at Illinois: you put your left arm above your left knee with your middle finger and your left ring finger tucked under. On one occasion, John thought he would be quicker off the snap by starting with both of his hands on the ground. He heard a voice.

"Three-point stance position."

John held his new, improved stance, eager to show the coach the results.

"Three-point stance position," the voice from above repeated.

Unfortunately for the young innovator, face masks were not yet part of the helmet in the late 1940s. A face mask might have prevented the bloody nose John received when Coach Dancey's foot met his backside and propelled him face-first onto the ground. At the time it devastated John. Later he rationalized that Coach Dancey wanted consistency in his players so they would learn to be confident, play better and do things right. Learn the fundamentals.

"I put my left arm above my left knee and tucked my middle finger and left finger and took my three-point-stance position for the rest of my football career," says John.

The Bert Dancey system paid off for the Flora community. Dancey's Flora High School teams won 177 games, lost 77 and tied 14 over his three-decade career. He ranks among the most successful coaches in Illi-

Bert Dancey won 177 games as coach for Flora High School over a thirty-year career.

nois high school football history.

John never played football again. He would continue to rise up the ranks of junior tennis and play basketball for Murray State. But the lessons learned from Coach Dancey in this three-sport small-town mecca would last a lifetime. There seemed to be a reason for everything. This is how we practice. This is why we practice this way. This is how the game is played.

John learned to play basketball left-handed because that's the way his neighbor played.

Chapter 4

FROG ISLAND

A combination of factors turned tiny Flora into a center for amateur tennis. All young men were expected to play three sports: football, basketball and tennis. Flora's oil discovery brought many families from Oklahoma and Texas, and they brought their love of tennis with them. Then there was the enthusiasm of Mr. Throgmorton and his travelling Flora tennis team. The local Catholic priest, the Reverend Monsignor John T. Fournie, shared this enthusiasm. John's father Cecil became known as one of the town's better young players.

Cecil and Mildred even carved out a tennis court behind their house. It became a gathering place for the youngsters of Flora eager to learn the game and just hang out. Cecil gave them instruction and, with the help of Mr. Throgmorton, made sure everyone had a racquet to play with. He also gave his young charges colorful nicknames, whether they wanted one or not.

Father Fournie built a tennis court on the empty land around the church. "He'd come out of the church, take his collar off, direct a tournament, put the collar back on and go into the church to conduct a service. After the service he'd come back out to the tennis courts and continue to run the tournament," says John.

"Flora probably has more people playing tennis per capita than any other city in the United States," Powless recalled to *Wisconsin State Journal* sportswriter Tom Butler in 1964. "They have lighted courts and about 100 kids 9 to 13 come out for

tennis three mornings a week."

When John started to demonstrate some ability on the tennis court as a teenager, Father Fournie would often drive John to tournaments.

"He would drive me five and half hours to Kalamazoo to play the national juniors, drive back to Illinois to do services and drive 350 miles back to Kalamazoo to pick me up," says John.

Back in Flora, Cecil formed what he dubbed the Frog Island Tennis Club.

"We'd hear all these frogs at night, so we called it the Frog Island Tennis Club," says Powless.

If you wanted to play at Frog Island, you waited in line on the grass that ran the length of the court. When it finally came your turn, you had to win your match or go to the end of the bench and start the process all over again.

Cecil Powless (second from left) with the traveling Flora tennis team.

"You would sit there all day long and you would play maybe four games," says Powless.

Flora in general and the Frog Island Tennis Club in particular had no shortage of colorful characters with even more colorful nicknames.

They called one guy Scaley Back Tolliver because it looked like he had fish scales on his back. He even worked carnivals in the summer and people paid a nickel to "see the human fish man."

Scaley Back's wife often found herself breaking up fights among the men in town. Often drunk, some of the men fought her back, earning her the nickname Hammer Head Tolliver.

Yellow Back Center and Baby Doll Fordsie often dropped by the Frog Island Tennis Club to check on the action.

Big Foot Mitchell claimed to work in the lawn care business. He would load his lawn mower on his trailer and drive into town, tie up his horse outside the saloon and drink all day.

"No one ever saw him cut any grass," Powless recalls.

The Bible-thumping duo of Ed Witherow and Elijah Pitts would come by the tennis courts and remind them that God blessed them, and then would retire to the tavern.

The Frog Island Tennis Club maintenance crew included mules that tugged a plow to shape the courts. When it rained, everything flooded.

John's father, Cecil, served as the unofficial mayor of Frog Island. His duties included awarding the coveted Frog Island nicknames. To earn a name, you had to catch a bullfrog in the middle of the night from nearby Coon Creek, where cotton-mouth snakes were known to slip in and out of the water. The ritual

The unoffical mayor of Frog Island holds court..

went something like this: A Frog Island tennis member armed with a flashlight helped the neophyte frog hunter with his or her catch. When the member shined the beam on a bullfrog, it froze. Once they froze a frog with the flashlight, the hunter would reach for the frog, but just as he was ready to grab it, the "helper" would inevitably move the flashlight and the frog would lurch to freedom. By the end of the night, the flashlight holder would eventually let the hunter catch his frog and earn his Frog Island name.

Even the city slickers who came to Flora to play in tournaments found themselves out along Coon Creek in the middle of the night trying to earn their Frog Island nickname. To this day, John Powless, who has played on virtually every tennis court surface in the world, says his fondest tennis memories come from the Frog Island Tennis Club.

Cecil Powless (third from left), Mr. Throgmorton (far right) and "members" of the Frog Island Tennis Club.

Today, all of John's eleven grandchildren bear a Frog Island nickname, although no one had to catch a bull frog in Coon Creek at midnight.

Chapter 5

CECIL

Tennis was not only a community affair; it was a family affair. When John wasn't playing at the Frog Island Tennis Club, he played or hit balls with his father.

"We hit tennis balls every day at noon and every day at five o'clock. And it was a given. He didn't say, 'Get dressed, we're going to play.' I was there," says Powless.

Cecil Powless taught himself how to play tennis. Before he married Mildred, he desperately wanted to date another Flora belle, but she didn't share the same passion for Cecil as he did for her. But she did tell him that if he could beat her in tennis, she would go out on a date with him.

"She beat the hell out of him," recalls John.

While the romance never blossomed, Cecil Powless set out to learn the game of tennis. He learned his serve from a flip book that animated the stroke of tennis legend Big Bill Tilden. He developed a strong enough game to earn a reputation as one of the better players in Illinois, if not the Midwest, competing against prominent national players like Bitsy Grant and Pancho Gonzales.

"I wanted to be there," says Powless. "To me my job was to do everything possible to get the ball back to him so he could hit it another time because he was the better player."

Outside of Flora, John's father was known as Cecil. But everyone in Flora called Cecil "Kayo." They called him Kayo after the actor Carl "Little Kayo" Erickson, who played munchkin herald #2 in *"The Wizard of Oz."* Drugstore custom-

ers would often watch Cecil disappear into the ice cream vats, reaching for a scoop of ice cream, and the name Little Kayo stuck. As Cecil grew older and taller, the townfolk shortened his nickname to Kayo.

Whatever they called him, Cecil Powless was a force on the tennis court.

"I remember when he once beat the Big Ten champion, who was supposed to be one of the best players in the country. My dad beat him decisively.

"Early on my dad would throw his racquet. I remember a game he played in the little town of Mt. Vernon, and the match finished and they shook hands and I said, 'You won.' He looked at me and said no, he didn't win, and I said you had to win because you didn't throw your racquet."

Cecil often used the tennis court as the family court. During one father-son session the junior Powless missed an easy shot and took out his anger on an innocent courtside bush.

"I just slashed this bush to sticks," says John.
When John went back to serve, there was no one on the other side of the court. Senior Powless had taken his racquet and gone into the house without saying a word.

Later that day, at five o'clock, John was ready to play again. But his father came out to the court, ignored John, and hit balls against the backboard, then went back inside the house.

"I told him I would never do that again. He accepted my apology and we played again."

Lessons learned on and off the Frog Island tennis court have stuck with John his entire life. Cecil entered John in

Cecil and Bob Powless

his first official tennis tournament when he was 11 years old. When John showed up for his first tournament, the tournament director asked him if he wanted to put on his shoes and shirt.

"I told him I played tennis barefoot," says John. The official then informed John that since he had neither shoes nor shirt he could not play. Since he didn't have a pair of shoes to wear at the moment the official disqualified John from his first-ever tournament.

When he wasn't trying to beat Cecil, he joined his father as his doubles partner at father-son tournaments. They would go on to win national father-son titles in 1952, 1957 and 1958. They even entered in 1973 when Cecil was 60 years old and made it all the way to the semifinals, where they lost to tennis legend Pancho Gonzales and his son.

"That son-of-a-gun could still hit the ball," John says of his doubles partner.

"I'd never say a thing to my dad. At some of these tournaments there would be fathers and sons screaming at each other. Sometimes one or the other father or son would get in some kind of snit and hit the ball way over the fence. I just ran over and got it and brought it back to play. I kept asking my dad, 'What's wrong with these people?' This didn't happen in my little hometown. Those kinds of people would have been exiled."

John's biggest fan was his mother, Mildred. Mildred ran the domestic side of the Powless clan, including washing everyone's tennis whites with a pump handle washer. She

John's biggest fan was his mother, Mildred.

played a pretty good game of golf but often found herself head cheerleader in the father-son showdowns at Frog Island.

"If my dad was playing cards a little late at night, she'd be on the fence saying, 'Beat him, beat him.' She was very supportive of all of this, and she'd be one who would express the emotional side of everything."

Even as John's game matured, the one guy he could never beat was Cecil.

"I was getting pretty good, so I thought I would win some games off of him. But in those years I could never win a game. It got so that we'd play against each other in the finals of a tournament and he still beat me 6–0, 6–0."

Cecil was quietly proud of his son's tennis game. Since Flora was an American crossroads, a variety of people passed through town on their

Cecil partnered with his son John in father-son tournaments until Cecil was in his sixties.

way to somewhere else. Now and again a traveler passing through would be armed with a tennis racquet looking to play this pharmacist Cecil Powless who was rumored to have some game.

"Up drives a man dressed in a suit and tie and says to my dad, 'I understand you play pretty good tennis.' Yes I do, says my dad. 'I'd like to play you,' says the city slicker. Dad replies, 'First you have to beat my kid.' "

The city slicker failed to qualify to play Cecil.

The one tournament Cecil never won was probably the one he wanted most: the Flora Open. In the 1930s and 40s the Flora Open—partly because of its easy access by train or car—attracted top players from New York, Boston, Miami and Los Angeles. It featured a 128-player draw and no tiebreakers and ran Friday, Saturday and Sunday from seven in the morning until they couldn't see the ball anymore.

"He never won it," says John. "I won it when I was 18 years old. That was a very emotional thing for him. But I still couldn't beat him. If he would have made it through the finals, I wouldn't have won it."

When you beat your mother or father at some contest, chances are you remember the first time for the rest of your life. That day came for John when he was a junior in high school. Cecil and John traveled to Matton, Illinois, for a United States Lawn Tennis Association–sanctioned tournament.

"I played a guy named Dick Savitt from East St. Louis, Illinois—supposed to be the best player around, number one seed—and I beat the guy decisively. And my dad played a guy from St. Louis, Missouri, who was the second seed, and my dad beat him in a long match. We played the finals and I beat him for the first time and then every time afterward. I thought that was the greatest thing in the world. I beat him 6–3, 6–1.

Cecil Powless poses with the sign that welcomes visitors to Flora and celebrates Cecil's and son John's National Father & Son Championships.

"We were driving back home in Mr. Throgmorton's car and I sat in the backseat with the largest traveling trophy in the United States. I was sitting beside this thing and I should be proud but I sat there and cried all the way home—60 miles and I cried the whole way because I had beaten my hero. It was devastating to me. To this day, I wish to hell I had never beaten him. I really do."

John Powless started beating a lot of players in his later teens. In 1951, his senior year of high school, he won the Illinois state singles title, beating the number two ranked junior player in the United States. Later that summer he played in the United States National Championships—today known as the U.S. Open.

Cecil and John would beat many players in and around Flora. One sportswriter dubbed the Central Illinois Tennis

Tournament the "Powless Tournament" because of the family's domination. Cecil won in 1947 and would come close many times. John won eight times from 1951 through 1958. John's younger brother, Bob, won it in 1963. John won in 1964 and Bob Powless won again in 1972. Another sportswriter called Cecil, John and Bob "one of the most famous Illinois tennis families."

"The Central Illinois Tennis Tournament was a big trip for us," says John. "To come out of Flora and go to Decatur and stay at a hotel—that was big-time. There would be 10 or 12 of us in one room because everyone from Frog Island would come."

John's brother, Bob, would go on to play as the number one player on the 1964 Purdue tennis team. Their sister, Kay, was a southern Illinois champion. John and Cecil would team to win the national clay court father-son tournament five years in a row, and even today, John teams with his son, Jason, to compete in similar father-son events. One of Illinois' most famous tennis families, indeed.

Chapter 6

THE U.S. NATIONALS

As an 18-year-old, Powless found himself among the better young amateur tennis players in America. But without much money, he was unable to play in many top tournaments. While associations often sponsored other top young tennis players, no such support existed in tiny Flora, Illinois. When he did venture out of Flora to play, he hitchhiked.

"When I'd go to tennis tournaments I'd walk out of my house and U.S. 50 and 45 were right there, and depending on which way I wanted to go, I stuck out my thumb and people would give me a ride," says Powless. "You'd hitch it. If I was in Chicago I took a train to Effingham, Illinois, that's 33 miles from my hometown. The train gets in at midnight. I'd walk a few blocks, stick out my thumb and hitchhike home in the middle of the night. That's what I did. I'd hitchhike to St. Louis, go north to Vincennes, Indiana, and hitchhike down the road to Evansville, Indiana, to play in a tennis tournament. It was me, my racquets and my bag."

As for European events: "It's a long swim and you can't hitchhike there," says Powless.

To actually make a living playing tennis in the 1950s, the top amateurs either accepted money under the table or turned professional. These professionals embarked on a series of tours. Bobby Riggs would play Jack Kramer, traveling from city to city over a period of a few months and playing before big crowds around the United States. They would play almost every night, collect the proceeds and move on to the

next stop on the "tour."

Most all the greats of those days turned professional in their early 20s. What this also did was ban these players from any of the so-called Grand Slam events: Wimbledon, the Australian Open, the French Open and what today is called the U.S. Open—all strictly amateur events, at least in theory.

It wouldn't be until 1967 when the "open era" arrived, allowing both amateurs and professionals to compete in the Grand Slam events. There is no telling how many of these events top players like Kramer and Riggs, Pancho Gonzalez and Fred Perry, Rocket Rod Laver and J. Donald Budge would have won if they had been allowed to play.

When John was 18, tennis hall of famer George Lott invited him to a tournament at the Edgewater Beach Hotel on Lake Michigan in Chicago. Lott had played in the 1930s and won most of his titles in doubles with a variety of partners. He won at the French Open, Wimbledon and the United States Nationals (now the U.S. Open) and played on two Davis Cup teams. He had heard of this young southern Illinois tennis player through his nephew, who lived in Flora.

Among the players in the draw was Seymour Greenberg, who had just won the Open Clay Court Championships. Powless went on to beat Greenberg in the finals. George Lott then called tennis great Billy Talbert in New York and told him he needed to invite this new young star to play in the U. S. Nationals at Forest Hills,

Tennis legend Althea Gibson helped John get ready for the U.S. Nationals. She won the Open in 1957 and 1958.

John took his big serve to the Big Apple the summer after he graduated from Flora High School.

New York.

Mr. Throgmorton footed the bill for the train ticket, and soon enough John Powless was in New York City, about to play the best players in the world.

"My neck got a little stiff looking up at all those skyscrapers," remembers John. "We only had two-story buildings in Flora."

Billy Talbert instructed Powless to go to the West Side Tennis Club in New York, stand near a spiral staircase and wait for a person to come and arrange for him to get some practice time. Talbert not only arranged for Powless to get some practice in, he lined up a young Althea Gibson, who was on the brink of tennis greatness, to be his practice partner.

Gibson would go on to win and win a lot, in 1957 becoming the first black player to seize the Wimbledon title. She defended her crown in 1958 and won the U.S. Open in 1957 and 1958 as well. She is best remembered for breaking the color barrier in tennis, and later professional golf, where she became the first African American member of the LPGA.

"So here's this kid from Flora hitting balls with the one and only Althea Gibson," says Powless.

Gibson was also a jazz singer, good enough to record a couple of albums.

An acquaintance from Flora arranged for Powless to get some additional practice at the prestigious Piping Rock Club on Long Island. Piping Rock is an old-money club, where members have dress codes for dining, golf,

tennis, squash and croquet.

Back at Forest Hills it was time for the tournament. The tournament directors had arranged housing on the grounds for those who needed it at $3.50 a night.

"My pillow," recalls John, "was a few feet away from the Long Island Railroad. My roommate was Mal Anderson from Australia. We couldn't get any sleep. So, in the middle of the night we grabbed our pillows and toothbrushes and crawled through a window at the Westside Tennis Club and we climbed to the top floor and slept on the bleachers. A big old German guy named Emil came in first thing in the morning to open everything up. We told him what we did and he said that's okay and put us in another room at the club."

Powless would face Mexican Davis Cup team player Mario Llamas in his first match his first time at the national championship. Llamas had earlier that year beaten Rod Laver in a Davis Cup match. The courts were packed with spectators.

"Mario said to me, 'You're nervous, aren't you?' I said yes, I was. He said 'Relax, either you're going to win or I'm going to win, and whatever happens, nothing bad is going to happen. So, just relax and play your game and you'll be fine.' We went out and I went up 4–1 in the first set and I'm suddenly relaxed.

"I'll remember a lot from my first experience—Mr. Throgmorton's generosity, Althea Gibson and what Bill Talbert and George Lott did for me. But I'll never forget what Mario Llamas said to me. It may be the greatest lesson of all." Mario Llamas also taught the young man from Flora a few things about tennis and beat Powless, despite John's early lead.

John (left) walks off the court after losing to Mario Llamas. Llamas played 44 matches for the Mexican Davis Cup team and taught John a valuable lesson he has never forgotten.

Chapter 7

MURRAY STATE

As a high school senior, John caught the eye of University of Michigan basketball coach Ernie McCoy. Coach McCoy offered John a scholarship, and soon he was on his way to Ann Arbor. Michigan seemed like a good fit for John. They had a new pharmacy school and he planned to follow in his father's footsteps.

After John's freshman year at Michigan, Coach McCoy left to become the athletic director at the University of Pennsylvania. Michigan hired Western Michigan coach Bill Perigo, who also coached high school basketball in Benton Harbor, Michigan. Coach Perigo told Powless that he could keep his scholarship, but Perigo planned to play only kids from the state of Michigan.

John's roommate at Michigan was Bobby Jewel from Indiana. It didn't take the two of them very long to convince each other to keep playing basketball, but to do that they both had to leave the University of Michigan.

"I gotta keep playing. I gotta go someplace where can keep playing basketball," John remembers Bobby saying.

John returned to Flora that summer and immediately received inquiries from Tulane, Miami, California and Murray State University in Kentucky.

Murray State coach Harlan Hodges knew of John Powless' basketball skill from a former player who had coached in Flora. Soon Coach Hodges was sitting in the

Powless family living room and, with a scholarship, invited him to come to Murray State. John accepted.

Part of Coach Hodges' pitch to Powless was the promise that he would play right away in his sophomore year. John could also

play on the Murray State tennis team, despite the fact that Murray State didn't have any tennis courts. To practice they marked off court lines with tape in the old basketball arena and used a volleyball net for the tennis net.

John with his doubles partner Art Smith, who went on to play baseball for the New York Giants. They never lost.

The tennis team included Johnny King, Brook Dunoy, Art Smith and Monroe Sloan. His college doubles partner was Art Smith, who later played baseball for the New York Giants. They never lost a match.

John never lost a singles match, either.

"You can say that the competition was questionable, but in my senior year we would go down to Florida State, Florida, Rollins College and play at the Naval Air Station, Pensacola. They were the top military tennis team in the country. Each campus had guys who were the top players in the country. Murray State would come to play and we had MSU and a big horse for a mascot on our uniforms and everybody would laugh. It didn't take them long to respect the horse."

For the young dual sport college athlete Murray State became an ideal place for the young man from Flora.

A typical Murray State day started with everyone
eating breakfast in the same cafeteria, followed by
class and chapel and ending with basketball or tennis
practice in the afternoon.

"The school assigned each student a seat in chapel.
It did not matter to the administration whether you
were class president, star athlete, straight-A student—
if you missed chapel five times, you were expelled
from school.

"One day a group of us decided to have a panty raid on the girls' dorm. The guys surrounded the women's dorm and the women are taunting us from the windows. President Ralph H. Woods shows up and says, 'Guys, I hope you have a good time. But if you set one foot on the grounds of this ladies' dorm you're going to be in Korea next week.' He just said 'Korea' and the crowd dispersed right away. We lived in the athlete's dorm and if you were caught in that crowd you were in big trouble."

Everyone chose Murray State over the Korean War.

The Murray State University basketball team. That's John, number 23 in the back row.

Despite its proximity to bourbon country, Murray State was in a dry county. "Thirsty" students had to drive the 20 miles south on Highway 54 across the border to Paris, Tennessee, to find alcohol.

"The white bar was Chief's. The Big Apple was the black bar. The team preferred going to the Big Apple because they also served barbeque rabbit and catfish. And because we were athletes we didn't want anyone from school seeing us drink beer. So we athletes went to the Big Apple. The room at the club where the white clientele went was about six feet by eight feet. They had a hole in the side of the wall large enough for a quart of beer to slide through. Because the room did not allow for too many white people, we also congregated outside when the weather was nice."

John, number 23, follows the play.

Not only was Murray State in a dry county, it was an all-white campus. All–white colleges were the

norm for the south in the early 1950s. As late as 1956 it was against the law in Louisiana for blacks and whites to mix at social events, including basketball games. Southern college sports teams didn't even recruit black high school athletes until Vanderbilt recruited Perry Wallace in 1966. Wallace became the first black basketball player to play in the Southeastern Conference—three years after Martin Luther King Jr. told the world about his dream. The University of Kentucky's first black basketball player arrived in 1970. "It wasn't integrated at all in the 1950s," says Powless. "We played in New York against Sienna and they had an All-American named Tim Hill who was black. I got to know him. We played tennis and he asked about the school because the high school all-star game was played at Murray State at the time. When Sienna came to play at Murray it was a major issue. When non-

John changed his number from 23 to 33 and is pictured here fourth from the left.

conference teams of color would come in, we'd shake hands, exchange a gift and embrace. After the Sienna game, a month went by before anyone outside of the basketball team spoke to me."

Some white coaches refused to play teams with black players. It was still more than 10 years before Texas Western, who started five black players, would upset the all-white University of Kentucky in the national championship game.

College basketball began to widen this small-town kid's view of the world. On his first airplane flight John said he fastened his seat belt, closed his eyes and tried not to open them until he landed.

He traveled to exotic places like Dayton, Ohio; Salt Lake City, Utah and El Paso, Texas.

Powless was an average-sized forward for his time, measuring six-feet-six inches. He eventually moved to the position of center. It was a new style of basketball for Powless: fast and tough.

"The coaches were great. In those days, everybody

BEVO FRANCIS

Bevo Francis is both a basketball legend and enigma. He scored 116 points in a game in his freshman year at Rio Grande and 113 points in a game in his sophomore year. Rio Grande expelled him for missing too many classes. He played for one of the patsy teams that "played" against the Harlem Globetrotters until he returned to his hometown and went to work at a mill.

pressed and everybody ran because that's what Indiana and Kentucky did. We played University of Texas El Paso, which had one of the first all-black teams. When you would go up for a layup, you had to carry two guys up with you as well as the basketball to shoot. You'd go up to the basket, one guy would separate your left hand, and another guy would separate your right hand, and they'd grab the ball and run down to the other end of the floor. You'd get knocked down; you'd get back up because you knew you weren't going to go to the free throw line.

"Our team didn't touch a basketball until November to get ready for the first game on December first. We didn't lift weights. We didn't run.

"There was no such thing as a training table. Nutrition meant if you were hungry and there was something in front of you, you ate it. If there wasn't, you had to find something.

"If there's contact today, you go to the free throw line. Back then, especially on the road, you knew you were going to take a beating. You knew you had to stand up after being roughed up.

"Once Coach (Harlan Hodges) called a time-out and said we had to change the tempo of the game. Nothing else was said. We came out of the huddle and I'm thinking, how are we going to change the tempo? All of a sudden this guy comes flying by me, hits the board and goes flying into the bleachers. My teammate Charley Sermons popped this guy in his nose. That one punch changed the tempo of the game. It turned into an all-out fight. No one on the other team came close to Charley Sermons again."

The rules of basketball also differed from today's game.

"There was no shot clock, so if a team didn't think they had a chance, they just held the ball. We played Memphis State and we held the ball because they held it on us when they came to our court. The Memphis fans in the stands started throwing coins at us. We couldn't get off the floor for a rebound because we stopped and picked up all the money

Murray State University today.

and put it in our socks. They didn't boo the next time we went to Memphis. They just threw coins, so we decided we'd make a little money, and we did."

Among the spectators of college hoops were the so-called pots and pans salesmen. In reality they were bookies and were ready to bet on just about anything.

"We were involved in a triple-header in Buffalo, New York. One of the games featured a player named Bevo Francis. He was recruited and was supposed to play at Murray State, but in the middle of the night one night he just got up and hitchhiked home. He wanted to go home, so he played for Rio Grande Community College in his hometown area while everybody in the world wanted him. The bookies would bet Rio Grande versus anyone. And then it would be Bevo Francis versus anyone. The bookies bet he would outscore the entire opposing team. He'd get the rebound and beat everyone else down the floor. He was a shooting star.

"In those days, a gambler would come and ask who the best rebounder on our team was, or who's your best guard. We'd point out two guys who had no chance of playing. The bookies took them out and got them tanked before we played St. Bonaventure, thinking they were disrupting our two best players. They would then bet heavily on St. Bonaventure and lose because those guys never played. We beat them."

The custom of point shaving became the preferred method for gamblers to manipulate games. The gamblers would secretly contact a player or two before the game and pay them to miss just enough shots to either lose or make the outcome of the game appear narrower than others had bet on. The outright throwing of a game brought their dealings to the attention of college governing organizations.

A point-shaving scandal made national headlines in 1951 when police arrested the nation's leading scorer, Sherman White of Long Island University. Authorities found more than $5,000 in cash taped to the back of his dresser.

"White said later that the toughest thing for him to do was to miss. Every time he took a shot he knew he was going to score," says Powless.

The point-shaving scam involved more than just the players, White told *The New York Times* in 1998. How could a coach not know something was amiss when his best players suddenly started playing poorly? White's Long Island University team was among the best, and they could almost control any game they wanted to. They succeeded by shaving points in the betting line. If they were favored by the bookies to win by seven and a half points, they won by one—winning both the game and the bet. Favored by four, they won by two, and so on.

White, who averaged almost 28 points a game, spent nine months in prison.

"He would have been the New York Knicks' first-round draft choice, but the NBA banned him because of his conviction," says Powless.

Because Flora, Illinois, is a day's drive from Murray, Kentucky, Powless seldom saw his family during his college athletic years.

"My family didn't own a car. They just couldn't get there. You only called home once a month. There was only one phone you could use and you called collect. In my hometown we still had the

John broke his neck in a basketball game in his senior year at Murray State. It was the last official basketball game he would ever play.

ringer. You had to go three long and two short to make a connection, and then 100 people could listen to what you had to say. You didn't call home very often because that was expensive."

On his first road trip he roomed with a Korean War veteran who had come to Murray State to play his final year and a half of college eligibility.

"We were in Houston. He said, 'Let's take a walk.' He turned to go into a bar and I said, 'That's a bar.' He said, 'I know it's a bar. That's where I'm going. Come on in.'

"I said, 'No, what if Coach sees us? He said, 'Come on in.'

"So we went in and that's when I found out what a shot and a snitch were. He had a shot of whiskey and a short beer. That night he had 33 points. I considered changing my training program."

Powless played all three positions for Murray State and began to attract the attention of more than one NBA team.

John Powless played basketball for Murray State from 1953 to 1957, until in his senior year, when he went up for a rebound and landed on his neck.

"I woke up a couple days later in the hospital with my arms and legs tied to the bed. Lucky for me a doctor named C.C. Lowrey came out of the stands and saved me. He put his thumbs in my head and pulled me. When we went to the hospital the ambulance wasn't long enough for me to fit in it, so the doctor sat on the tailgate to keep my neck in place.

"My room was on the far end of the hospital near the fire escape. My buddies would go down to the Big Apple in Tennessee and bring the beer and barbequed rabbit up the fire escape to my room at midnight."

The doctors first fitted him for a cast around his neck. As he healed, a harness replaced the cast. He had trouble accepting that he could no longer be part of the team and soon could be found at the gym shooting baskets with his upper body still in the harness. The doctors told him his competitive sports days were over. Yet by that summer, he was back on the tennis court. He had sniffs from NBA teams and was offered a tryout with the Cincinnati Royals. Somehow, Dr. Lowrey—the same doctor who had come out of the stands and saved his life—had heard of this offer. He reached Powless by phone and warned him that one more injury to his neck would either put him in a wheelchair for life or kill him. Powless took the doctor's advice and never played competitive basketball again.

"I did everything to get ready but thought if I get hit again, I'll be in a wheelchair. I told them I wasn't coming."

Lucky for him, he still had tennis.

When Powless arrived at Murray State in 1953 they did not have tennis courts, let alone a tennis team. Powless helped Murray State field a team. He entered the year's Ohio Valley Conference tennis tournament without playing a single regular-season match.

"We washed cars to get the money," says John. "We had just enough to get to the tournament and back home. But it rained the final day and the tournament was postponed. We had no motel to stay in and ate baloney sandwiches and drank Coke for dinner and breakfast. We lost the conference meet by a point."

Powless distinguished himself in tennis at Murray State. He ranked as the number one amateur player in Kentucky. He never lost a regular-season singles or doubles match. He reached the NCAA quarterfinals twice and the semifinals once, and the team finished fifth in the country in 1956. He was the Ohio Valley conference singles champion all three seasons he played. He shared the conference doubles championship three years in row and later became a charter member of the Murray State Hall of Fame for tennis.

Here's what sportswriter Bill Carter wrote about the Murray State ace:

"Murray State's tennis team is powered by the brilliant John Powless and three Paducah netters. John has put Murray State on the tennis map. Although forced to struggle through last season without sufficient funds in a new sport, Powless turned down scholarship offers from several major colleges which field strong tennis teams.

"He kills you with a vicious but accurate serve and demoralizes opponents with his grace and crisp play on the court. More people around here should see this big guy in action."

After graduation in 1957, Powless entertained overtures from the U.S. Naval Academy and the University of Miami about coaching basketball and tennis. Since neither position would be available until the fall of 1959, he went back to Flora and worked with his father in the pharmacy. He had to work somewhere because by the time he graduated from Murray State he was married to Delores Heater and they had a son, John, in 1956.

John's first postcollege job away from Flora was teaching math at Paducah Tilgham High School—the largest senior high school in Kentucky. He coached cross-country and assisted with the basketball team.

In the spring of 1958 he traveled to Florida to play in the Masters tennis tournament. On his way back to Paducah, he stopped to visit the athletic department at Florida State University in Tallahassee. The FSU athletic director, Perry Moss, knew Powless could play tennis because FSU had lost many matches to him and Murray State. Now they asked him if he'd like to join the faculty and help coach the tennis and basketball teams. He became head coach in tennis and assistant to Bud Kennedy in basketball.

"They said, 'We've got all these great facilities but only a few tennis classes.' So once I came on board we grew the tennis classes to more than 40 a year."

In 1958, FSU was primarily a women's college, although since the end of the Korean War, more men had arrived on campus. The athletic facilities at FSU were among the best in the country, with an abundance of tennis courts, bowling alleys and swimming pools.

One of his first jobs after Murray State was coaching the Florida State tennis team. He also assisted the basketball team. That's John back row, left.

During his Powless' tenure at FSU there were no African American students. Even the black janitors that were hired to clean couldn't come onto campus until after dark.

"I would come back to campus at night and set up a tennis ball machine indoors to practice against. The guys would come in to clean and I got to know them. The head guy was Willie. He and his crew would fish all day, come in to clean at night. I played pool with those guys and shot buckets. They'd retrieve balls for me and I got to know them really well."

While at Florida State he played tennis with John Coatta, an assistant football coach who would become a lifelong doubles partner and friend. Coatta would leave Florida State to become the head football coach at the University of Wisconsin in 1967, where he reunited with Powless to form a doubles team that few could beat.

Powless' coaching curiosity and scouting efforts led him to nearby Florida A&M. Florida A&M was as black as Florida State was white. Powless was often the only white person in the gym.

"They were phenomenal," Powless says of the Florida A&M basketball players. "They flew up and down the floor, running up scores that would make the NBA jealous."

While southern social protocol prohibited Florida State from playing Florida A&M in the regular season, Powless wanted the Florida State team to play at least a few practice games against them.

"The Klan dropped by one day and said, 'Don't take your basketball team over to Florida A&M to practice because they have blacks.'"

Integration, when it was allowed, came quickly to FSU in the form of their basketball team.

"At that time, as good as they were, they couldn't fill up the little gym that sat 3,600 people because the team was black," Powless recalls. "Whites made up most of the rest of campus."

Murray State's tennis practice facility was the gym. The team taped lines on the floor and converted a volley ball net to serve as a tennis one.

Chapter 8

UNIVERSITY OF CINCINNATI

During his coaching days as assistant at Florida State, Powless took a call from the University of Cincinnati asking him for a scouting report on one of the teams FSU played regularly. Teams help each other with scouting reports even today. He sent his report, and soon afterward Cincinnati's new head coach, Ed Jucker, called.

"I'd sure like to meet you," Powless remembers Jucker saying.

Powless didn't think much of the call at the time. After all, one of the greatest players to play the game, Oscar Robertson, had just graduated. At best, Powless figured, Cincinnati would be rebuilding.

Powless went to Cincinnati to play in a tennis tournament not long after his conversation with Ed Jucker. On a whim, he walked the few blocks from where he was staying up to the athletic office, where he found Coach Jucker, a piece of chalk and a blackboard.

"About three hours later I'm choking on chalk dust. We talked about what kind of offense we ran and this and that. We talked about the science of jump balls."

Once the chalk dust had cleared, Powless returned to the tournament to play his match.

"I was playing in the semifinals at the first major grass tournament of the season in Philadelphia. I was in the locker room and I got a phone call. And I would never take a phone call before a match but for some reason I took it. It's Ed

Jucker. 'I'd like for you to come be one of my assistant coaches.' We didn't talk about salary or anything. I said, 'Fine, I'll do it.' It was one of the best programs in the country. Donald Dell, who would later create Pro Serve—the number one sports talent agency in the United States—asked me what the phone call was about. I told him it was none of his damn business.

"We were walking from the locker room—being escorted into the stadium to play our match. Dell stopped and said, 'It's over with in Cincinnati. Oscar left. There's no more basketball there, John. What are you doing? You're crazy.' "

How crazy? Oscar Robertson was a three-time All-American. He left Cincinnati as the leading scorer in college basketball history. He led the U.S. Olympic team to the 1960 gold medal. He was a star in the NBA and is considered one of the greatest players to ever play the game. John knew all of this, and he still decided to go to Cincinnati to become one of Ed Jucker's assistant coaches.

As the young John Powless joined Ed Jucker's staff of two to coach basketball, he would also find himself with a front-row seat to racial history.

Oscar Robertson was the first black athlete to play basketball for the University of Cincinnati—an almost all-white university. But Cincinnati would soon become one of the most integrated basketball teams in the country, thanks in part to the success of Robertson and the recruiting of Oscar's coach, George Smith, and his

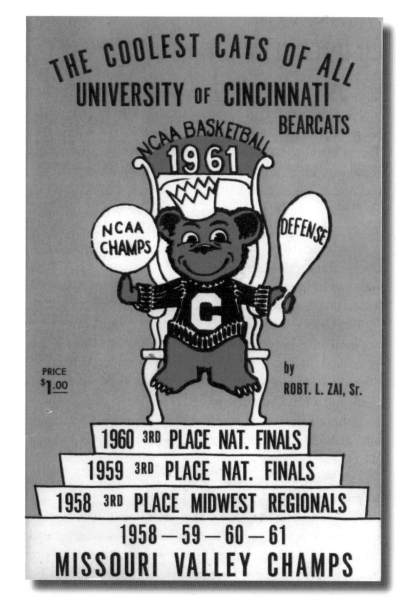

successor, Ed Jucker.

Ed Jucker described himself in an article for *Sports Illustrated* as "a man who has paid his dues." He played baseball and basketball for Cincinnati, served in World War II and coached high school basketball before returning to his alma mater as an assistant to Coach Smith.

Smith had transformed the Cincinnati basketball program, and it didn't hurt that he had one of the most prolific scorers and all-around players in the history of the game in Robertson. But as Donald Dell had reminded Powless, the Big O was gone.

And while Robertson opened the door for other black players, none of his successors on the Cincinnati team had his skill. No one in the world did.

So in walked Ed Jucker, Tay Baker and John Powless into a new era of Cincinnati basketball, into an arena of Bearcats fans who were now used to winning—and winning in the high-flying manner led by Robertson. Robertson's team had raced up and down the floor scoring 90 or more points a game, with the Big O scoring a third of them.

But Jucker decided he couldn't play that style with his current roster. Instead he implemented what would become known as Cincinnati power basketball: No mistakes, good defense, control the game, work as a team.

The fans hated it and booed the team and Jucker for this new methodical style. *The Cincinnati Enquirer* wrote, "Life without Oscar Robertson is going to be difficult."

Cincinnati lost three of their first eight games. The team that had been the toast of the town for the past three years was putting everyone to sleep.

But it was basketball, basketball and more basketball for the 25-year-old John Powless. He arrived at the basketball office every morning at eight. He and his fellow assistant, Tay Baker, watched film to break down opponents and study their own team. Then he would get to practice. After dinner he would attend a high school game to scout new recruits.

When the 1960–1961 season began, the Bearcats struggled. They lost three games in seven days, including a game against Seton Hall that gamblers had fixed. Cincinnati couldn't even beat the team that gamblers were paying to lose. Coach Jucker sent his assistants to the film

Coaches Powless, Jucker and Baker celebrate after beating Ohio State for the 1962 NCAA basketball championship.

room to find out why.

As with many in his profession, basketball consumed Ed Jucker. He liked to say he coached like he played, and he played all-out all the time.

Powless remembers his boss as straightforward and serious. He raised his voice only to referees, and no one recalls ever hearing him cuss. But during games, Jucker's Dr. Jekyll transformed into Mr. Hyde. He would leap off the bench, screaming at officials so much that his players and assistants had to restrain him. He said he was just so into the game, he didn't know what overtook him.

Once in practice, when Powless did cuss out one of his players, Jucker quietly told him to find other words to get his message across.

Then, eight games into the 1960–1961 season, a switch flipped in the Cincinnati locker room and the Bearcats started winning—slowly and deliberately—but winning. The Bearcats won 19 games in row and made it back to the NCAA tournament. They beat Texas Tech and Kansas State to reach the Final Four in March 1961.

"Who's the first one to call for tickets? Donald Dell, the man who told me it was over at Cincinnati."

The following year, they beat Ohio State again to win the 1962 championship.

"One thing Jucker did was really make you feel you were the most important person in the whole

John Powless, head coach Ed Jucker and assistant Tay Baker, the staff at the University of Cincinnati basketball team.

program," Powless says about his mentor.

Part of any assistant basketball coach's duties is scouting upcoming opponents.

"I scouted our NCAA opponents all three years. I learned the meaning of work under him. He spent endless hours and used every available practice period and every available hour preparing for practice and games."

While basketball dominated his life 10 months a year, Powless still played tennis tournaments in the summer. Professional tennis in 1960 was virtually nonexistent. Apart from the major tournaments—the French, Australian and U.S. Opens and Wimbledon—events were hosted outside any official governing body. The United States Tennis Association had only a room, a phone and not much money.

But the good tennis players still made money. Event organizers attracted top players by paying them under the table.

"They'd take us out to the golf course, throw a ball down two inches from the hole and say, 'I'll bet you two hundred dollars you can't make that putt.' They might squeeze a few bucks in your hand at the trophy presentation, but it wasn't much."

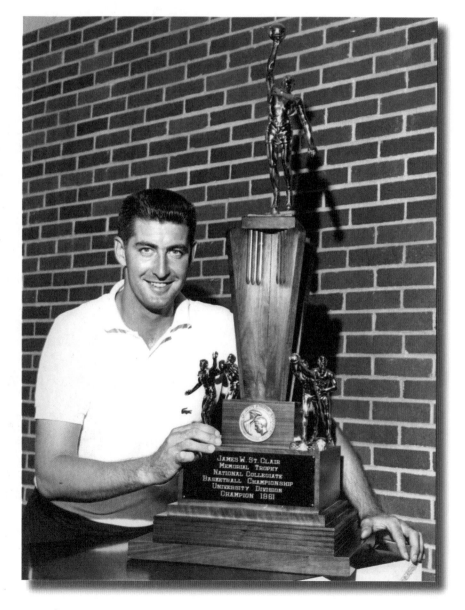

Chapter 9

THE KATZENJAMMER KIDS

While Powless was at Florida State, Billy Talbert (pictured here with John) called him one day and told him to go to a New York City hotel to meet a man. The man was Harry Hopman, an Australian, who was arguably the most influential tennis figure of the time. Harry Hopman had won as a player, once taking the Wimbledon mixed doubles title with his wife, but he became a tennis legend as a coach and teacher.

"There was no fooling around with Harry Hopman," Powless says.

Australia dominated world tennis under Harry Hopman, especially when it came to the Davis Cup.

The Davis Cup began in 1900 when four Harvard players suggested a match against a team from Great Britain.

One of the Harvard players, Dwight Davis, organized the format and contributed a trophy. They called it the International Lawn Tennis Competition, but as the competition expanded to other countries, it became known as the Davis Cup. The Davis Cup became the gold standard of international tennis competition, and in the 1950s Australia ruled this tennis world.

Harry Hopman won 16 titles as a player and captain. It certainly helped having Aussie greats Roy Emerson, Rod Laver and Neale Fraser representing your country.

Roy Emerson would go on to win eight Davis Cups and 28 career Grand Slam titles, a record that stood for 36 years until Pete Sampras surpassed Emerson.

Some call Rod "The Rocket" Laver the greatest player ever. He won his first Grand Slam as an amateur. In 1959, Hopman brought his Australian Davis Cup team to New York City to play the United States. Since World War II the United States and Australia had dominated the Davis Cup, with Australia winning a majority of years. Hopman needed fresh sparring partners for his team and sought some of the better non-Australian players, among them John Powless.

"I got involved as a sparring partner with the Australian Davis Cup team," says Powless. "That was Emerson, Laver and Frasier—the number one player in the world at that time. About the same time a guy named Tom Price out of Cincinnati asked me what I would do if I had the best juniors in America. I said we would get up in the morning and run. We would practice. We would play matches. We would practice in the afternoon, run again, do light weights and start over the next day. And we would do it every day."

In other words, he would do what he saw Harry Hopman do with the Australians while borrowing a few techniques he learned from Coach Dancey in Flora. Little did Powless know at the time, he would soon get the chance to put his ideas into practice. Soon, in addition to playing the summer tennis tournaments, Powless found himself coaching what would become, in effect, the junior members of the U.S. Davis Cup team. His job was to round up the best-ranked American junior players ages 15 to 18 and take them on the road to compete in some of the better tournaments around the country.

The first player was Dennis Ralston. Ralston would become the number one ranked male player in the United States three years in a row. Dennis Ralston became the youngest player in history to win a Wimbledon crown in doubles. He also won the doubles crown at the French Open and the U.S. National Championships. He ranked number one three years in a row. He played on the Davis Cup teams from 1960 to 1966 and captained the team from 1972 to 1975. He won three Grand Slam titles.

John Powless (far right) with a bunch of skinny teenagers, who would become some of the greater names in the game in just a few short years. Six went on the represent the United States in The Davis Cup.

With Ralston and seven more of the top juniors crammed into Powless' Buick, they traveled the south in the heat of the summer.

Powless would apply much of the same discipline he'd learned as a boy in Flora: Go and go hard all day long. He had the teenagers up early, hitting balls, playing matches after lunch, studying other matches, running on the nearest golf course at night, followed by light weight lifting before bed. Not everyone among the reigning powers of organized junior tennis agreed with their coach's approach to training. Today it's called cross training, but connecting weight training with hitting drop shots was far from most traditionalists' thinking.

By the end of the summer, the young men crammed into Powless' Buick beat most comers and beat them badly. His young players were on their way to becoming the biggest names in American tennis.

Charlie Pasarell from Puerto Rico became the number one ranked player in the United States in 1967. He played on five Davis Cup teams, including the championship squad of 1968. He won 18 singles titles and the U.S. National Indoor Championships in 1966 and 1967. Pasarell won the NCAA singles and doubles championships while at UCLA in 1966.

Frank Froehling and Clark Graebner also played on the Davis Cup teams that won four titles in a row. Known for his big serve, Graebner teamed with Dennis Ralston to win the 1967 French Open doubles title. Charlie Pasarell would go on to win major titles. But in that Buick, all were sweaty teenagers barnstorming the country on the road to greatness.

"We looked like the Beverly Hillbillies," their leader recalls. "Rolling down the road, three in the front, five in the back with all our gear and suitcases tied the top of the Buick."

When they did get to stay at a motel, all eight stayed in the same room, alternating who slept on the bed and who slept on the floor. Many nights a bag of hamburgers served as the training table. Many of these young men became multimillionaires later in life, but as teenagers they were living the sweet life playing tennis and seeing America from the back of a Buick.

The best junior in the world at that time was Bill Lenoir. He could beat anyone on clay courts, but in those days ranking points came mostly on grass courts. The boys reached the U.S. Open Clay Court Championship in Chicago and promptly won five of eight matches against the current U.S. Davis Cup team, and the tennis world took notice. Sportswriter Bill Jauss labeled Powless' band the Katzenjammer Kids—a popular newspaper comic of the day—in the Sunday *Parade* magazine.

The United States Lawn Tennis Association—the governing body of American tennis at the time—endorsed the juniors program but didn't give them any financial support. At that time the USLTA barely had enough money to keep a phone on a desk at 128 East Broadway in New York. The only employee that director Lawrence Baker employed was himself.

"They were better off losing the Davis Cup in Australia and earning $50,000 in consolation money than hosting the

Davis Cup in the United States and winning," says Powless. "They couldn't draw enough fans in the U.S. to pay the bills to host the event. Australia could fill a 30,000-seat arena for a Davis Cup match. The United States could give tickets away and still not fill a multi-thousand-seat venue."

So Powless and his merry band of boys on the road stayed in private homes, ate breakfast with their hosts and conducted clinics for local kids to get practice time. The hosts of the clinics made money from the busloads of kids eager to pick up a few tips from the eight best junior men's tennis players in the country.

Eventually road conditions improved. Billy Talbert found a way to get cars from Studebaker. Money for gas and food came from the clinic organizers.

Some members of the first U.S. Junior Davis Cup team included Dennis Ralston, Clark Graebner, Marty Riessen, Frank Froehling, Bill Lenoir, Ramsey Earnhardt, Bill Bond and Charley Pasarell.

Also among this group of early elites was Arthur Ashe, who would become the biggest name in all of tennis. This Richmond, Virginia, tennis phenom learned the sport in a blacks-only park, where his father worked. The job came with a house right in the middle of the park, and that's where Ashe first played tennis. When he wasn't reading or earning straight As in school, Ashe turned the heads of the best black tennis players in America. This eventually led to the interest of Dr. Walter Johnson, who became Ashe's lifelong teacher and mentor. Dr. Johnson demanded more of his students than a great overhead smash. Aside from tennis, Ashe learned about work habits from Dr. Johnson, like cutting the lawn and painting the fence.

Arthur Ashe

Ashe soon started winning junior tennis tournaments. As the color barriers faded in his high school years, he traveled to where the best juniors played and beat most of them most of the time. One summer, he joined Coach Powless' traveling Junior Davis Cup team.

"He never questioned a call," says Powless. "He never raised his voice or threw his racquet. His intellect became his greatest asset. He was hardly the strongest player of his day, but he was head and shoulders the best."

One stop on the tour that summer was Southampton on Long Island in New York. The players all had places to stay, and the last player Powless had to drop off was Ashe, who had been assigned to servants' quarters for lodging while the rest of the team stayed in houses. Powless was nonplussed, and so, despite the protest of young Arthur (who had grown up in the segregated South), he arranged for the entire team to stay together—together or not at all.

This photo dated February, 1963 thanks John for his "tremendous leadership and sacrafice in bringing these and other youngsters to the realization of our objectives, challenges and aspirations." That's John far left.

Ashe went on to star at UCLA and become the first and only African American male to win the U.S. Open, the Australian Open and Wimbledon. He played on the U.S. Davis Cup team and would later serve as captain. He was a founder of the Association of Tennis Professionals, the organization that developed professional tennis into the sport it is today.

Ashe wanted to do more than play tennis, and that part of his life began while he was the number one ranked U.S. player in 1969. He applied for a visa to travel to South Africa to play in the South African Open. This was the apartheid South Africa that had thrown the most popular opponent of its racial policy, Nelson Mandela, in prison for 25 years. South Africa denied Ashe's request. He applied the next year, and South Africa denied his request again. After several denials, Ashe urged the International Lawn Tennis Federation to expel South Africa's membership, a move that would effectively ban any South African from international competition. The ITF, as it's known today, was and is the governing body of international tennis. In 1973, when South Africa finally granted Ashe a visa, he told the organizers he would come, but only if black youth worked among the other ballboys and ballgirls. Ashe became the first black athlete to compete in any national sporting event in South Africa, reaching the finals in singles and winning the doubles with Tom Okker. He also requested a visit with the still-imprisoned Nelson Mandela. Years after his incarceration, when Mandela first came to New York, the first person he went to see was Arthur Ashe.

Ashe and Powless remained in touch throughout Ashe's career. On February 6, 1993, Powless was in Detroit to substitute for Ashe and speak at an event. While in the airport, he was approached by a stranger who said he was sorry to hear about his good friend. In his usual manner, Powless thanked the stranger, having no idea who he was talking about. As he walked farther down the terminal, he caught sight of a television monitor. Arthur Ashe had died of AIDS, which he'd contracted through a blood transfusion. He was 49 years old.

"If we don't continue to work for the things he stood for, then he's gone forever. But if we do, he will live forever," Powless says.

While Powless will always remember his future tennis stars as "good kids," on more than one occasion, if the player's conduct was not up to the coach's standards, Powless would walk onto the court in the middle of a match and tell the umpire the match was over. How a player conducted himself nested in the core of the Powless philosophy—on and off the court. When a player left the home of someone who had hosted him for a tournament, Powless required him to leave a flower and write a note, which Powless would mail from the road. Perhaps his lessons on chivalry influenced a young Arthur Ashe, who, Powless remembers hearing, insisted on answering his own fan letters.

This team of young players and their exacting coach changed the way the USTA (having dropped the "Lawn") groomed its players for international competition. For the first time these talented individuals joined a team. They practiced together. They watched matches together. They traveled together. They ate together.

"When there were problems with an individual, they would talk as a team," says Powless. "Do you want to be part of this or not? Make up your mind right now. If you do, we've got a bag of hamburgers waiting in the car. We're going to Chattanooga."

For most of them, most of the time, it became an experience of a lifetime, and the team spirit transformed into lifelong friendships.

"I remember when the scrawny 15-year-old Mike Belkin was the best junior in the world. Fresh from beating the 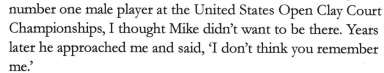 number one male player at the United States Open Clay Court Championships, I thought Mike didn't want to be there. Years later he approached me and said, 'I don't think you remember me.'

"Yeah, Mike I do.

"He came up to me with tears in his eyes and said those were the greatest years of his life. It's too bad I didn't realize it then. Before those guys were 20 years old they were our Davis Cup team. They won, and they won with class."

Skinny little Mike Belkin is now the tennis pro at the Sonesta Beach Hotel and Tennis Club in Key Biscayne, Florida.

When one of his future tennis stars displayed more bad attitude than good tennis, Coach Powless wasted no time in yanking his young star from center court in a packed stadium in a crucial match—defaulting the match. After assuring a stunned umpire that defaulting the match was exactly what he was doing, he drove his troublemaker to the airport, sweaty tennis whites and all.

"You have to clean up your act," Powless told him. "You can't play again until I say you can play again."

Clark Graebner found himself on the receiving end of a

classic Powless "this is how we behave in this universe" lecture. Graebner cleaned up his act enough to become a successful professional tennis player, reaching the number one ranking in the United States. He would play with and against Arthur Ashe. He played on the U.S. Davis Cup team from 1963 until 1970. He was known as one of the most powerful servers in the game and won the 1966 French Open doubles title with Powless grad Dennis Ralston. His record in Grand Slam events is 108–58 for a 65 percent winning percentage. When his daughter married, Coach Powless attended the wedding. When Graebner saw Powless there, he started to cry. He would tell people at the reception that Powless was the most influential person in his young life.

Today the USTA has several youth development programs, but John Powless led the first. The organization paid Powless a total of $100 for five summers. During one of those summers, Powless played in the U.S. Southern Open. He won, and the name John Powless is on the trophy along with Pancho Gonzales, Fred Perry, Bobby Riggs and Jack Kramer. He became the third-ranked doubles team in the United States with partner John Skogstad. They would make the prestigious round of eight in the U.S. Open.

John in New York City with Jimmy Schaefer and Mike Belkin, two of the top junior players in the United States.

Chapter 10

CINCINNATI V. LOYOLA

Without a chance for a steady income playing tennis, once school started at Cincinnati, Powless headed back to Ed Jucker's staff and prepared to win a third national championship in a row.

"We believed if we won three national championships in a row, we were going to be the Olympic coaching staff in 1964," says Powless.

Cincinnati marched through the 1963 season and once again made the NCAA tournament. They drew a bye in the first round and went on to beat Texas in the round of eight by five points and Colorado by seven points and again found themselves in the Final Four. They embarrassed Oregon State in the semifinals and faced Loyola-Chicago in the final.

Winning two championships in a row had shed the college basketball spotlight on Ed Jucker and his staff of two. Both assistants received feelers from other programs about the possibility of getting their own head coaching jobs. University of Wisconsin athletic director Ivan Williamson called Powless and asked him to visit Madison to talk about the possibility of coming to coach at Wisconsin. North Carolina State and Florida called as well.

While Wisconsin tried to get a meeting with Powless the weekend of the Final Four (Cincinnati's fifth in a row), the young assistant had more pressing issues. While preparing for the final, the bulb on the film projector fried. Powless went scrambling to find a new one. As Powless rounded the corner

of the hotel lobby, Ivan Williamson from UW approached and asked him if he had time to visit. This time Powless promised that once the game was over, he'd meet with the Wisconsin delegation. Powless procured a projector bulb from the local photo shop, raced back into the hotel and was next approached by Davis Cup player Barry MacKay. MacKay had no coaching offers; he just wanted to know how much Cincinnati would win by that night so he could get a bet down. MacKay's traveling partner was tennis legend Jack Kramer, and the two were ready to see Cincinnati go for three championships in a row. After finishing his film preparation for the championship game, Powless heard what Wisconsin had to say. Wisconsin's coach at the time, John Erickson, wanted a change, the delegation told Powless. Would he have any interest in becoming the next head coach?

Meanwhile Tay Baker—Powless' fellow assistant—was also entertaining head coaching offers. After all, Cincinnati found themselves at the doorstep of winning three NCAA basketball crowns in a row, something no school had done before. They had to be doing something right. Cincinnati came to the tournament with a 23–1 record, playing Ed Jucker's Cincinnati power basketball: stingy defense, few mistakes and fouls (the lowest number in the country) and solid team play. Little did anyone know at the time, the Loyola-Cincinnati game would become part of NCAA lore—part basketball and part civil rights.

In 1962, Cincinnati had become the first college team to start four black players. As the Civil Rights Movement heated to a boil, Ed Jucker broke an unwritten rule at a time when some teams still refused to play against teams with any black players.

That same year, an African American man named James Meredith had tried to enroll at the University of Mississippi, touching off days of rioting in which two people were killed. By 1963, Americans watching the nightly news had seen police dogs attacking black residents in Birmingham, Alabama, where also, under the supervision of Theophilus Eugene "Bull" Connor, firefighters sprayed black protesters with fire hoses. Martin Luther King Jr. delivered his "I Have a Dream" speech before a quarter of a million people in Washington, D.C. And, as at Cincinnati a year earlier, Loyola coach George Ireland started four black players. When the only white player fouled out in a game, he substituted another black player, making Loyola the first team in college basketball history to play five black players at the same time. Cincinnati dressed an integrated team as well. It was the first time an NCAA championship game featured more black players than white.

A sellout crowd crammed Freedom Hall in Louisville to watch the most powerful offense in the country in the Loyola Ramblers play the land's most suffocating defense in the Cincinnati Bearcats. For the first time in history, a national television audience watched an NCAA final in the tournament that today has become a national three-week

A restored page from the 1961-62 University of Cincinnati program. Note John lower right as coach of the "Bearkittens," UC's freshmen team.

festival. Loyola's powerful offense took the floor and proceeded to miss 13 of their first 14 shots, eventually missing 26 of 34 shots in the first half. Cincinnati opened a 19–9 lead and by halftime led 29–21.

After the half it was more of the same—Cincinnati scoring, Loyola laying bricks. Loyola started to press in a desperate attempt to claw back into the game. Despite Loyola's relentless press, Cincinnati rolled out to a 15-point lead. But Cincinnati also racked up fouls, letting Loyola back in the game. Conventional basketball wisdom suggests that the team that presses commits the most fouls, but as the game wore on, it was Cincinnati who found their star players sitting on the bench in foul trouble. Of concern to coach Ed Jucker and his assistants was that one referee was calling most of the fouls in the second half—on the same team that led the nation with fewest fouls per game.

For the final 13 minutes of the game, Loyola whittled away at the Cincinnati lead and with 12 seconds left found themselves down by a point, 53-52. Cincinnati's Larry Singleton stood at the free throw line. He sunk the first basket. One more free throw and it would be impossible for Loyola to overcome a three-point deficit in 12 seconds (the three-point basket was still years away from becoming part of the game). Singleton missed, igniting one of the most remarkable 12 seconds in sports. Loyola's Lesley Hunter rebounded the miss and fired a pass to Ron

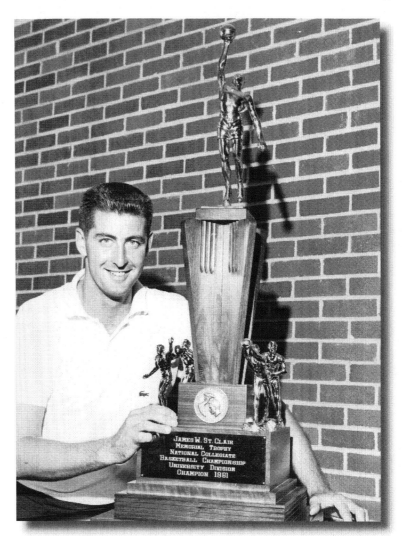

Twenty-nine year old John poses with the James W. St. Clair Memorial Trophy for the 1961 national championship.

Miller, who fumbled the ball and, to the shock of everyone in Freedom Hall, traveled. The evidence is on the film—not just one extra step but several. Yet neither referee, Alex George or William Hussenius, blew the whistle to call the infraction. Miller regained control of the ball and passed it to Jerry Harkness, who hit a shot to tie the game with only six seconds left. Jucker tried to call a time-out, but his players couldn't hear him. The 1963 national championship game headed to overtime for the first time in tournament history.

"Miller somehow made it across the 10-second line without dribbling—an obvious traveling call that went without a whistle. We were sick to our stomachs," says Powless. "What took at least 10 seconds in real time somehow took less than three seconds in basketball time."

Overtime went back and forth, and after a last-second tip-in, Loyola won by two. In an aching defeat, Cincinnati lost its bid to become the first NCAA basketball team to win three straight championships. After the game, Powless sat alone in the locker room, growing angrier each time he replayed the last few seconds of the second half in his head. Before he accepted the offer to come to Wisconsin, Powless sat alone again, this time obsessing over the film. Like virtually all good coaches of high school and college sports, Powless endlessly replayed game footage to try to determine what went right and what went wrong. But this was the last game of the season, and while Powless knew it might be his last at Cincinnati he felt compelled to take one last look at what he felt was a crime scene. This time, he fumed.

While there is plenty of speculation about what happened that night, one theory suggests that the Big Eight officiating crew wanted legendary Oklahoma State head coach Henry Iba to lead the 1964 Olympic basketball team. If Cincinnati won, the job would almost have to go to Jucker. Not long after Loyola clinched the NCAA tournament title, the U.S. Olympic Committee announced that Iba would lead the team.

Despite the heart-wrenching outcome, Cincinnati will always hold a special place in Powless' heart. He might not have known it at the time, but he was an eyewitness to and participant in the beginning of a new era in college basketball. Racism in sports would continue, but the 1963 championship game between Loyola and Cincinnati became a landmark event. To this day, Powless continues to stay in touch with many of the players. They all graduated (as did Loyola's starting five), and all, according to Coach Powless, have been a positive influence in their communities. A few have passed away, as has the head coach, Ed Jucker.

With the 1964 season in his rearview mirror, Powless accepted the offer to visit Wisconsin. During his visit, the Wisconsin athletic department threw a party at the Westside Businessmen's Club. Powless loved the camaraderie and was especially impressed that the staff did all the cooking and tended bar. It sealed the deal, and Powless let Ivan Williamson know he was ready to become the next coach of the Wisconsin basketball team. He was 31 years old.

*John and mother Mildred about the
time John moved to Madison.*

Chapter 11

BADGERS

Ed Jucker lasted two more seasons at Cincinnati and then suddenly and unexpectedly resigned. The job, he declared, was too demanding, and his family was complaining that he hardly knew his four children. He was hospitalized for an appendectomy and had kidney problems and a cyst, which had to be removed. His passion for the game was killing him.

When Powless had accepted Williamson's offer, it was with the understanding that the team's current head coach, John Erickson, would still be on the payroll. His suitors assured him that Erickson would be moving into an administrative position before the start of the next season. With a job in hand, Powless hit the road to play tennis tournaments for the summer. When he arrived on the Madison campus the following September, the basketball secretary told him that Williamson wanted to see him immediately.

"He said, 'Coach, close the door.' I thought I was getting canned even though I'd only been there for 12 hours," Powless recalls.

Instead, he was told that John Erickson had decided to stay. Williamson asked if Powless would take the job of assistant coach with the basketball team—and head coach of the tennis program. Given that it was too late in the year to go anywhere

else, Powless accepted Williamson's new offer.

Powless' first year as an assistant started poorly. The Badgers' center and one of their best players became academically ineligible. Wisconsin won only two conference games, finishing dead last in the Big Ten.

Life as an assistant wasn't much different at Wisconsin than it had been at Cincinnati. The assistants did everything. They went to games together. They scouted high school players together. They watched film together.

Powless loved every minute. He had arrived at a school that ranked among the better teams in one of the better conferences in the country. The Big Ten had more Final Four and championship teams than any other conference.

The arena, however, preceded today's basketball palaces. The Badgers played at the aging Field House—the type of facility universities built to accommodate a variety of events, from student registration to graduation to boxing matches and even horse shows. The basketball team played on a portable floor that was set on dirt. The roof leaked. Powless and his fellow assistants often used towels to soak up the puddles after a late-winter snowmelt. In the fall, the basketball team often shared the Field House with the football team.

Yet Powless soaked up the coaching culture. It was an era when head coaches stayed with the same school a long time, whether they won or not. The coaches from opposing schools spent time together. They went out to dinner together the night before the game.

The demand for revenue did not exist in 1960s college sports. Today's head coach supplements his and his assistants' salaries with camps, shoe deals and radio and TV shows. There were none of these when Powless arrived in Madison. He can't remember the exact number, but Powless figures he made about $8,500 as an assistant. He would have coached for free. He loved the air he breathed and the game that produced it. Once he arrived in Madison, he never thought of living anywhere else.

John Erickson, the head coach who was supposed to fade into retirement, kept coaching, and Powless spent five years as an assistant basketball coach and the head tennis coach.

John recruited Joe Franklin, who became the Badger's all-time leading scorer.

One of the first things he did when he arrived was look in Madison's backyard for a skinny kid from the since-closed Central High School. His name was Joe Franklin, and Powless was the only one who thought he could make it in the Big Ten. In his three years with Wisconsin, Franklin scored more points than any Badger in history.

Between seasons, Powless packed his racquets and tennis bag and hit the road to play a few tournaments: the Blue-Grey, the U.S. Southern, the U.S. Open. The United States Lawn Tennis Association (now the USTA) ranked Powless as high as 25th in singles and sixth in doubles among U.S. amateurs.

Back in Madison, the day finally arrived when Coach Erickson did what he said he would do five years earlier, though this time he left Madison altogether to become the general manager of the new Milwaukee Bucks NBA team. Later Erickson would run unsuccessfully for the U.S. Senate.

UW basketball staff: Assistant Dave Brown, head coach John Erickson and assistant John Powless.

Instead of offering the job to Powless as promised, the athletic department conducted a search and instead offered the job to the young Army coach, Bobby Knight. Knight accepted and asked UW to wait before making the announcement until he had time to contact Army. As the head coach at Army, Bobby Knight was in the army. No one will know how Knight planned to convince the general to let him out of the army and go to Wisconsin. It didn't matter. The story leaked to *The Wisconsin State Journal,* and when Knight learned of the leak, he called UW to decline the offer on April 28, 1968.

That same day John Powless became the head coach of the University of Wisconsin basketball team. If he was concerned about being the school's second choice, he never said so.

"Actually, so many people called to give their condolences when Knight got the job, and they called again when I

1972-73 media guide cover

got it. I don't feel I'm second choice to them."

He inherited a team that had finished fifth in the Big Ten the year before. Or, as one local sportswriter put it, a program that was both "mediocre" and "colorless." The writer also pointed out the run-down condition of the Field House and how there were no words to describe the condition of the locker room.

"We had running water in the locker room," says Powless. "It ran along the floor when the snow started to melt in the spring.

"One day this guy came running into my office yelling, 'I just called the fire department, the roof is on fire!' All I said was, 'Why did you call?'"

Here's how radio broadcaster Ira Fistell described the state of Wisconsin basketball in the official 1972 media guide: "The state of Wisconsin has a relatively small population, and its high school basketball, while improving, does not rival scholastic programs in Illinois, Indiana, Ohio or Michigan. The University has little basketball tradition. The weather was (and is) cold. The physical facilities were not only old, they were shabby: the field house roof leaked, the floor was dead, and the locker room facilities had best be left undescribed. Finally, Wisconsin's periodic campus upheavals cause more than one parent to send his son to more passive if less socially committed institutions."

That from the official media guide.

With an uphill challenge on a variety of fronts, recruiting the better high school players from the Mid-

*John is carried off the floor after his Badgers upset
nationally ranked Kansas 67-62.*

west became Coach Powless' top priority. Because of the head coaching uncertainty surrounding Erickson's plans, those better players went elsewhere.

Powless took over Wisconsin basketball at about the time other schools in the Big Ten started building new, modern arenas. Then, as now, opposing coaches would use anything they could to lure the best high school talent.

"If they (opposing coaches) had the opportunity to use the Field House against you, they did," Powless notes. Powless tried to counter this facility liability by bringing recruits to campus on homecoming weekend, when the Field House became one large, loud party. He'd tell the recruits that if they thought it was loud then, they should hear the place during a basketball game.

The noise in the Field House did make a difference in many close games before, during and after Powless. But between games it could be one big, empty barn—a barn you did not want prospective players to see.

"Sometimes we could only hold half-court practices because the other half was flooded," says Powless. He also inherited a growing anti–Vietnam War campus environment that gained a national reputation for its demonstrations. Opposing coaches kept scrapbooks of news clippings on Madison and made sure the top high school prospects and their parents had the opportunity to look through them. It's not that their parents didn't already know. The so-called Dow Chemical riots on campus the preceding fall, October 1967, had made news everywhere. While UW–Madison was not the only college that featured antiwar protests, it certainly led the league in publicity. Television news networks showed the dramatic scenes of student and nonstudent protesters being beaten and sprayed with tear gas. The protesters had virtually shut down the university.

The Vietnam War peaked at about the same time, but the public's support of the war faded. Bobby Kennedy and

Eugene McCarthy announced they would run against the incumbent president, Lyndon Johnson—a fellow Democrat. In a few weeks President Johnson told America he would no longer seek his party's nomination. A few weeks later, in April 1968, James Earl Ray assassinated Martin Luther King Jr. In June, Sirhan Sirhan killed Bobby Kennedy after Kennedy gave a speech celebrating a presidential primary victory.

And for a new coach about to take the most important job of his life, it became harder and harder to attract high school basketball stars to even visit the Madison campus. There were days when players could not get through crowds of antiwar protesters to practice. Other days they waited for the effects of the tear gas to subside before they could leave practice. They left for road trips five days before the game just to have a safe place to practice. Protesters sometimes circled the Field House so fans and players couldn't get in. Once the team had to remove the screens from the back windows of the Field House, run out into the football stadium (attached to the Field House) in the snow and enter the arena from the rear.

"Another time we entered through the showers and the coaches' offices because the paddy wagon blocked the door," says Powless.

"Sometimes we would practice in front of 8,000 people. They were from the National Guard and other law enforcement agencies called to campus by Governor Warren Knowles to help keep the peace. They bunked at the Field

Kim Hughes (number 45) and his twin brother, Kerry were overlooked by every college coach in America except John Powless.

House or the natatorium. The players and the Guard often ate dinner together."

A new coach brings new promise for fans, and the 35-year-old Powless did not disappoint. After losing the season's first game to Nebraska, Wisconsin faced nationally ranked Kansas. Few, including some pessimists on the team, believed Wisconsin could beat this national powerhouse.

After a couple of players chuckled when Powless told his team they could beat Kansas, Powless offered them an alternative.

"There was a sort of lackadaisical air with two or three of them," he says. "I told them if I don't have all the guys who believe we can win, they should get dressed and go sit in the stands."

When Wisconsin upset Kansas 67–62, giddy fans picked up their new coach and carried him off the floor. Co-captain James Johnson told the *Wisconsin State Journal* after the game: "Coach Powless is such a wonderful coach. He got us sky high for this game. I wanted to win so badly. I thought nothing but basketball from the time I left the court Monday until after the game."

Johnson scored 29 points in the upset. The *State Journal* called the occasion "one of the school's most important athletic achievements in years."

The rest of that first year went up and down. His first team finished with 11 wins and 13 losses and tied for eighth place in the Big Ten. They played eight teams ranked in the top 20 and beat four of them, including third-ranked Kentucky as well as fourth-ranked Kansas.

One star player ignored the demonstrations and agreed to transfer from the University of Florida to Wisconsin. Tony Miller was an outstanding yet unhappy sharp-shooting point guard. Legendary Indiana coach Branch McCracken suggested he visit the Badgers, which he and his father did in August 1970. Everything seemed to go well with admissions and academic requirements, and the Millers were scheduled to meet Powless for breakfast in their hotel to finalize plans for Tony to join the Badgers.

Earlier that morning, on August 24, 1970, a van loaded with 200 pounds of fertilizer blew up outside Sterling Hall on the UW–Madison campus, killing a young researcher, Robert Fassnacht. The bombing, intended for the army research building next door, not only made international news, it abruptly ended the Millers' interest in the University of Wisconsin.

"I went to breakfast with the bombing on the front page of the newspaper and the Millers never showed up," remembers Powless.

"Phone calls weren't returned. I never heard from him again. Add that kid to our team that was ranked and who knows what would have happened?"

It might have been the worst day of his coaching life and maybe his worst birthday ever. John Powless was 38 years old.

Too busy to spend too much time licking wounds, Powless pushed forward. His team rules were simple. They were the same ones that worked for his father, Cecil, and Coach Dancey in Flora, and they would work for him in Madison: treat everyone the way you want to be treated. If you can't say something nice, don't say anything at all. The most serious violations come from a person who has all the ability but doesn't play hard.

Despite the campus turmoil that he would never blame for his performance as a coach, Powless dressed some good teams. He recruited Kim and Kerry Hughes from Freeport, Illinois. The Hughes twins were relatively late bloomers in high school and pretty much ignored by other Big Ten programs. As sophomores on their high school basketball team they played guard. But that next summer they grew seven inches—so quickly that they developed other physical problems, including fatigue. Kerry Hughes said they slept 14 hours a day during their growth spurt.

They were tall and getting taller, but they were unknowns when it came to college recruiters. In fact, despite their growth spurt, they didn't even play much their junior year. That changed after the next summer, when the twins be-

Fans flood the floor and raise their new coach John Powless on their shoulders after the Badgers upset nationally ranked Kansas 67-64. A player told the newspaper after the game: "Coach Powless is such a wonderful coach. He got us sky high for the game. I wanted to win so badly." The newspaper called the game one of the school's most important athletic achievements in years.

came stronger, pumping weights in their backyard and gas at their father's Sunoco gas station. They were tall, fit and much better basketball players by the time their senior year rolled around. But still, no interest from recruiters. John Powless was among the uninterested, even though he coached a Big Ten team only an hour and a half from Freeport. But he was also a relentless recruiter. If you could play basketball in America, John Powless knew your name, your high school coach's name and where you lived.

He found and recruited the Hughes twins almost by accident. He knew of a talented player in northern Illinois named Mark House and drove the hour and a half from Madison to Freeport to watch him work. But it was the Hughes twins on the opposing Freeport team that really caught his attention. By now the twins averaged about 15 points and 15 rebounds a game—impressive statistics for 32 minutes of high school basketball. Mark House became Mark Who and Powless offered scholarships to Kim and Kerry Hughes to play for the Badgers. Powless could barely contain his excitement, as his new recruits were six and a half feet tall and still growing. The twins grew five more inches by the end of their senior year.

The arrival of two 6-foot-11-inch players excited Badger basketball fans and drew national attention. In February 1974, the twins posed for the cover of *The Sporting News,* the most influential sports publication of its time, with the headline "Wisconsin Twin Towers." That team ranked as high as 13th nationally and by today's rules would have been a high seed in the NCAA tournament. Unfortunately, in 1974 only the Big Ten champion earned a bid.

Some people thought Powless was too nice to coach. Tom Butler of the *Wisconsin State Journal* called him

When you are a college coach, everyone has advice for you, even your mother.

Kerry Hughes and his identical twin brother, Kim were drafted by the NBA.

charming but also "intense" and sometimes "caustic."

"He drives himself incessantly," Butler wrote.

Despite his nice-guy reputation, Powless would sometimes padlock the doors of the Field House to keep the media and other people out of practices. He admits to having been out of control at times. He emphasized being thorough. Just as he had done at Cincinnati, his staff looked at films of opposing teams all day long and sometimes through the night. They wanted to know if a player took two dribbles left and came back to his right. They wanted to know what defense they ran. They wanted to know what they had for breakfast. Powless wanted his players to know. He loved preparation and hated time off. To the coach, playing on the team was an extension of the overall educational experience of being a student.

"Prepare here and you'll be prepared for success after college and basketball," Powless says. "All I had to sell was the University of Wisconsin and the scholarship the player would receive to play."

While he had to compete with the protest climate of the university, he also recruited against coaches and programs that used cash to attract the better players. Some players and their families charged up to $10,000 just to let a coach visit a recruit's home. If you don't believe this, Powless says, you're naïve.

"You knew it was there," says Powless. "Coaches who recruited with cash were trying to be competitive with everybody else. There were guys who claimed to be clean and there were guys with great programs who would say I know something's going on, but I don't want to know anything about it.

"When a school racked up multiple NCAA violations, it wasn't because they bought a kid a hamburger and a Coke. They had air travel, cars and apartments. We're not blowing the whistle on anybody. That's the way the game was played, and I think it still is in some places. How are you going to trace cash? How are you going to put the finger on somebody who did that?"

Instead of bribes, Powless offered a top-notch education and the chance to play big-time basketball—a mantra and a legacy that live on in Badger men's basketball to this day.

One year, Powless and coaching colleague Fred Taylor of Ohio State conducted a study of the NBA draft, which in those days could last for 30-plus rounds. Back then, NBA teams drafted almost every Division I college basketball player. The pro teams hedged their bets that some unheralded player would blossom into an NBA star. What they found is that only one percent of the players drafted by an NBA team made an NBA roster. Of that one percent, only one percent played in the NBA long enough to draw a pension.

"So you ask kids, 'Why are you going to school?' If you're good enough to make that elite one percent, that's terrific," says Powless. "But you'd better get an education just in case you end up in the other 99 percent."

He told potential recruits' parents that they would have a great experience at Wisconsin despite what they read in the newspaper or saw in the news.

"We'll watch after your kid. If your kid gets sick, he's going to be in our house until he gets well (a supposed NCAA rules violation). He goes hungry? He's going to be in our house for a meal. We're going to check in with the professors every week to make sure he's attending classes. If he's not, we're going to find out why. We're going to treat your son just like he's ours. We're going to take care of him, and we can't promise any more than that.

"When we had a married student with a kid, my wife and I would babysit so the couple could go out to a movie. It's all against the regulations. When did we stop being human beings and having a little civility?"

One year during the Powless era, six of the 11 Badger players made the All-Academic Big Ten team. Most everyone graduated.

Years later, Clarence Sherrod—pound for pound the best player Powless says he ever coached—stood next to Powless in the middle of Camp Randall Stadium as the two were being honored at halftime of a Badger football game for their induction into the Wisconsin Sports Hall of Fame.

"Clarence leaned over and said he was sorry they didn't win more games for me," says Powless. "I told him he played as hard as possible all the time and that's all we asked you guys to do. You always tell young people to just be yourself. But if you need an outlet, you can always blame me."

Clarence Sherrod finished his career at Wisconsin in 1976 with 1,408 points—breaking the mark set by Powless' first recruit, Joe Franklin.

A lot of what Powless taught, he says, he learned from Coach Dancey.

"There's a right way and a wrong way. Once we settle on the right way we'll do it a hundred times. You had your responsibility to the other players to do your job. And that was it."

Ask Powless to pick his favorite players is like asking a parent to pick their favorite child.

"Yes, there are certain players that you sort of embrace more than others because it wasn't so

Coach Powless at Camp Gray: (left to right) John, Kim Hughes, Dave Van Mueller, Lamont Weaver, Lee Oler and Brad Sherman.

much that they didn't give you problems, it was like they got it. They got it right away," says Powless. "Some you can scold. Some you can shake a little bit. The others, even though they make a thousand mistakes, you have to pat them on the back like they did nothing wrong. Some of those teams that didn't win as many games as the others might stand out more in your mind because of how hard they played. They had their own egos and their own pride to play."

As for his official record of wins as head coach, it was the tale of two schools for John Powless. For three years as an assistant at Cincinnati the team won 78 of 84 games. As the head coach of Wisconsin, Powless' teams won 88 games and lost 108.

Yet despite his record at Wisconsin, no one wanted to play a Powless-coached team: Not Bobby Knight (Indiana), not Fred Taylor (Ohio State) and certainly not Al McGuire (Marquette).

"John Powless just plain outsmarted me," McGuire told a writer.

His Badgers played the second game ever at the new Assembly Hall in Bloomington, the new home of Indiana basketball. Notre Dame lost the first game 92–29. Powless told his team that when they hit 30 points he would call time-out to celebrate. They did, and he did.

"Bobby Knight came storming over and said, 'What the blankety-blank are you doing?' I told him we were celebrating setting the new scoring record for a visiting team." Knight said congratulations and went back to the bench. Wisconsin won the game.

Anyone who takes coaching seriously does more than tell players what to do. They live it.

"You wake up in the middle of the night in a cold sweat and you say, 'God, we have got 39 minutes and 40 seconds gone in the game and we haven't scored yet,'" as Powless recalls a recurring nightmare. "But I loved it all."

If there is a single tenet to Powless' coaching philosophy, it is to treat each player as an individual. Find his or her strengths and exploit them. He never wanted to expose a player in the areas in which they struggled. If the player can shoot but can't play defense, find ways to get him the ball and "hide" him on defense.

"It builds confidence. Take the weak defensive player. You never tell him you're putting him on their weakest player. You tell him that his guy is important and keep him from getting to the basket. Even though you know that guy doesn't go anywhere anyway. You don't tell the kids that. You want them to feel very, very important."

THREE BLIND MICE

Legend has it that Powless once led the University of Wisconsin band in a version of *"Three Blind Mice"* during a basketball game to complain about the officiating.

It's a great story, only it's not true.

Minnesota came to Madison to play but dressed only 10 players. Teams carried 15 players, but in an effort to control costs, the Big Ten allowed 10 on road trips. During the game, one of the players drew three fouls in the first half (five and a player is disqualified) and a fourth at the start of the second. Short on players, the Gophers coach kept the player in the game. Powless ordered his team to "go inside" and try to get the player his fifth foul.

"We went inside again and again, but no foul was called," says Powless. "It was pretty obvious to the crowd and me that the guy was fouling, but the referees didn't call anything. The crowd was upset. I was upset. I was pacing up and down the sideline, waving my arms trying to get the refs' attention. About that time bandleader Mike Leckrone was so upset he ordered the band to play *"Three Blind Mice,"* and the next thing I know I'm accused of leading the band in the song when all I was really doing was trying to get the refs to blow their whistles. The band was on the other side of the gym from the bench."

The next day athletic director Elroy "Crazy Legs" Hirsch issued Powless a letter of reprimand.

Says Powless: "Elroy told me he was required to give me the letter but said, 'Look, I understand. Don't worry about it.'

"Years later I was in Maui with the Big Ten commissioner, Wayne Duke, and he was telling UCLA coach Jim Harrick how I stood on top of the scorer's table and led the band in *"Three Blind Mice."* He told Harrick that I went all the way down the floor to lead the band. This is the commissioner of the Big Ten adding to and embellishing the story."

In 1998, the year the Wisconsin basketball team left the UW Field House for the brand-new Kohl Center, the athletic department invited Powless and others to attend the last basketball game in the old barn.

Lamont Weaver, John and Dave Van Mueller.

"I went up to the three refs and told them that they wanted me to lead the band in *"Three Blind Mice"* at half-time," says Powless. "I asked if they would join me. It's the last time at the Field House. They said sure, it would be fun.

"Here comes halftime and the PA announcer said, now we'll have a reenactment of the infamous playing of *"Three Blind Mice,"* and me and the three refs went in front of the band and the four us conducted the band.

"The league went crazy. But what were they going to do to me, because I'm not coaching anymore? I did get a phone call from the league office the next day asking how could I do that. You didn't ask our permission. I told them I didn't realize I had to ask their permission and if they played the game again tonight, I'd probably do it again.

"Here, the former commissioner was telling the story. He thought it was funny. Jim Harrick thought it was hilarious. Even after Harrick left UCLA and coached at Rhode Island, he told the story to one of his assistants before we broadcast the game: 'He's the guy who jumped on the scorer's table and led the band in *'Three Blind Mice!'*' "

The legend gets better and better every time someone repeats it.

John with his future father-son doubles partner, Jason in 1971.

The 1975–76 season started well enough for the Badgers. They beat Marquette, they beat Ohio State and were ranked in the top 20 in the nation. But injuries took their toll, and the Badgers limped through the Big Ten season winning only four games and finishing ninth in the league.

John Powless could not remember a basketball season when he wasn't either playing or coaching. That changed when athletic director Elroy Hirsch and John Powless met in Hirsch's office after the 1976 season. After eight years, Powless left UW–Madison. Powless was 44 years old.

Despite the change at Wisconsin, Powless remained a respected coach among his peers, and when other coaching opportunities surfaced, Powless' name was part of a school's conversation. One of his biggest fans was Johnny Orr. As coach of the University of Michigan men's basketball program, Orr won more games than any previous coach in the program. Then he quit and left for Iowa State.

"There were opportunities to go to other schools," says Powless. "Orr tried to get me to do it, and when people would call him when there was an opening at a school he would call me and say, 'They have got an opening at such and such a place.' And I said no thank you. I think I have had my time."

Coaching college basketball is much more than teaching your team how to win basketball games. Above, John runs a camp in Managua, Nicaragua. Left, he takes his turn in a dunk tank at a Madison community fundraising event.

Chapter 12

COACH ON COACHES

Despite leading opposing teams, coaches have a special fraternity. Head coaches may have served together as assistants in another program on their way up the career ladder. Coaches will talk to each other about the problems they experience. Coaches invite other coaches to watch and evaluate team practices. It's as if everyone knows at some point in their careers that they will need one another.

John Powless has his favorites.

AL MCGUIRE

While the fraternity of coaches was strong when Powless was in the game, there were still plenty of rivalries. One of the best in the country was Wisconsin versus Marquette. John Powless versus Al McGuire.

The Wisconsin-Marquette rivalry started in football, when Marquette had a team. The school suspended the football team in the early 1960s, and a basketball rivalry picked up where the football one left off. Separated by little more than an hour on Interstate 94, both schools recruit the better players in the Midwest. There are bragging rights issues. If you live in Milwaukee and you root for a college football team, it's likely Wisconsin. If you live in Milwaukee and you root for a basketball team, it's likely Marquette. Many closets in Milwaukee hold team

colors of both schools worn in accordance with which school is playing which sport on a particular day.

The public and media saw Powless and McGuire as rivals. The two coaches saw each other as friends, often meeting halfway between Madison and Milwaukee to talk about coaching and life into the wee hours of the morning.

The games were sometimes classics, as in the Milwaukee Classic of 1970 when the second-ranked Marquette needed a last-minute bucket to beat Wisconsin. McGuire, who often struggled to control his emotions, jumped on the scorer's table to express his joy after the game. The crowd loved it, except for Glenn Hughes, the father of Wisconsin's Hughes twins, who saluted McGuire with an extended middle finger that was immortalized by a Milwaukee newspaper photographer. The newspaper removed the middle finger before publishing the photo, although versions of a "restored" photo have surfaced. In the foreground of the photo, Powless is seen walking off the court with his head down. Marquette finished the year 28–1, losing to Kentucky by one point in the NCAA tournament.

"If present-day television coverage existed back then, those would have been *the* games," Powless guesses. "They would be great on TV because you have got overtime, double overtime, last-second

RALPH MILLER

"I always thought one of the coaches a lot of people wouldn't know is Ralph Miller." Powless first met Ralph Miller when he coached at Wichita State and Powless coached at Cincinnati. From Wichita he went to Iowa, while Powless coached the Badgers in the Big Ten.

"I thought he might have been as good as anybody that I had been around in my 20 years of Division I basketball," says Powless. "He knew his kids and the kids bought into it because they knew if they did, they would play. They knew Miller's way gave their team a chance to win. He had a year when he was 0 and 14 and comes back the next year and he is 14 and 0. And he had only added one player to the group. That's pretty good coaching."

Ralph Miller not only turned around the Iowa basketball team, he set Hawkeye fans on fire with a team that averaged 103 points a game and jammed the old Iowa field house. He did more of the same at Oregon State. He retired in 1989 as the seventh most successful coach in NCAA history.

shots and plenty of emotion.

"It was a rivalry, but it was a greater friendship. The day he arrived in Milwaukee I happened to be there. And the athletic director said, 'You know our new coach is here and I would sure like for him to meet you.' And I said fine and we did. Not too long after that first meeting, we were doing some basketball camps together. We did TV shows together. Al was a good friend. I mean I truly miss him because he would give me a call at nine o'clock at night. And he'd say, 'I've got to talk to you. I've got to visit with you.' We would meet halfway in Jefferson. I'd get in the car in Madison and he would come from Milwaukee. And we would be sitting there all hours. And we would go back home.

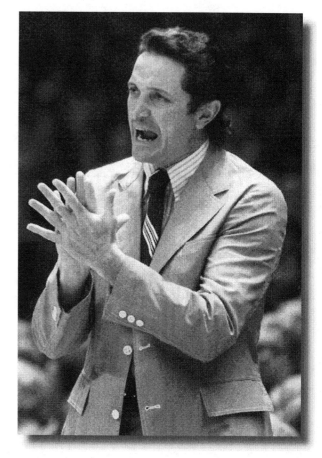

Al McGuire

"Probably the alumni of both places would say, 'You know, this is not good.' His teams could run up and down the floor. He had a medium tempo. He could slow it down. He could play any way he needed to win. But the thing is he was trying to get a kid in position. One of his kids could jump like a helicopter. He could get up in the air and stay there forever. Couldn't shoot worth a lick. But his role was to get under the basket and stay there. And so he did. His job was to keep the ball away from the basket and he did.

"Al succeeded because he understood his players. The ability to go out and get the players that you wanted is one thing. You can't always do that. That is the downfall of many coaches. Everybody knows who you would like to have. Al was able to do that. He would fill the role he needed filled.

"Coaching was Al's stage. He was really completely different away from it. We walked around the lakes up in St. Peter, Minnesota, where we worked a basketball camp in the summertime. We'd walk around the lake and talk about things and the monks would be walking around doing their meditation. We were right in the middle of them.

"One thing he said often, privately and publicly, is that he wouldn't want to be in the Big Ten. He would have to play those teams every week, every night that we play. He wanted tough games. But he also wanted three or four where he could mix things in and experiment a little bit with his players. Is that smart scheduling? No, that is smart coaching. He knows if every night was a tough time then he may have some kids that might break down. He was successful enough for long enough and he had his kids believing they could beat anyone."

After Marquette and McGuire knocked on the NCAA championship door more than once, they won it in 1977. Al McGuire had a good cry in the locker room and never coached another basketball game. It surprised everyone except John Powless.

"In coaching you can lose your life. You can lose your own personality. Didn't surprise me one bit. To win it was one thing. He already knew he was leaving.

"Here comes Al after a tough night on the road and he gets off the plane and tells his wife that he can't go home yet. He has to talk to one of his kids. It's one o'clock in the morning and he's got to talk to them. If he waits until tomorrow it may not get done. And he goes right to where the kid lives because he is going to sit down and talk to him. Every successful coach works that way. And it isn't necessarily the basketball game. It is their life that is going to be well beyond their years in basketball. Basketball is an extension of the educational program. If we win some games, so much the better."

There are two titles that seem to stick to a person long after their duties expire: governor and coach.

"I didn't think much about it when I was coaching, but now, later in life when somebody says, 'Hey Coach, how are you doing? What did you do to prepare for the games?' If people look at me and they say 'coach,' it makes me feel good. Maybe I did contribute a little bit.

"Or a former player gets married. They have kids. Or they have a tragedy. You contact them. Or you make a surprise visit to one of your guys that is working on a doctorate degree. And the guy breaks down crying when you show up in the room. You say, you know, maybe, just maybe a coach had a little impact on them."

Al McGuire and John Powless remained friends long after they coached against each other. When McGuire became a successful broadcaster of college basketball games for TV, he often called Powless for any insider information he might use in the broadcasts.

John last saw his friend in the hospital right before Al McGuire died on January 26, 2001, at age 73.

BOBBY KNIGHT

John Powless first saw legendary coach Bobby Knight when Knight, the player, came off the Ohio State bench to play against Cincinnati.

"In the second national final he got to play because we were up by 20 by halftime," Powless likes to joke, noting when Cincinnati beat Ohio State.

Like Powless, Knight continued in basketball as a coach, first at Army and later at Indiana, where he earned his legendary status. The two became friends, swapping game films and enjoying a steak the night before their teams competed against one another. In between games, there were countless phone conversations. Powless learned the Robert (as he's always called him) far apart from the "General" label others put on him.

One thing about Knight that Powless learned right away: he never really cared what anyone thought of him. He cared about his players and the game of basketball, in that order. Most college basketball fans know about the time Knight threw a chair across the floor, the time he kicked a player or when he was accused of choking a player in practice. But Powless says there is much more to his friend Robert than his public persona.

"A guy with terminal cancer wrote Robert and asked for an autographed picture. Robert got the picture but didn't autograph it. Instead, he drove to his house and knocked on the guy's door at 11 o'clock at night. They sat and talked until sunup. When he left, he asked the guy if he'd still like to

have the photo and the guy said he did. And he signed it in front of him and gave it to him.

"He drove back to Bloomington that morning for a coaches' meeting."

Powless would also like people to know how committed Knight was to his players. When they left Indiana and later Texas Tech, Coach Knight would tell them he was always available for whatever they needed. Need help finding a job? Coach Knight will make a few calls for you.

Powless remembers when Knight asked a former player how tough it was for him at Indiana. The player, a walk-on who had to pay his own college expenses, admitted that it was indeed very tough until Knight gave him a scholarship.

"He said, 'Coach, I never knew how I was going to buy my next book. Where the next meal was coming from. Tuition. But I was good enough you put me on scholarship the last two years and that was good," says Powless.

Later, the player called Knight and asked for tickets to an Indiana game, which the coach happily provided. When he reached his seats he was surprised to see Knight's wife waiting for him.

"She said, 'Here, Coach wants you to have this,' and she handed him an envelope. After she left he opened it and found a check equal to the cost of his first two years of college."

It's almost as if his good friend is playing Bobby

BRANCH MC CRACKEN

Indiana's Branch Mc-Cracken had the luxury of picking from an Indiana high school basketball crop that, at the time, was the most fertile in the country. Every Indiana kid played basketball, just like in the movie *Hoosiers*. And every kid wanted to play for Branch McCracken.

"They would throw the ball into the air and it was up and down the floor," says Powless. "He knew his talent was going to win. Indiana would let you score 20 while they scored 30. Indiana could do just about anything they wanted."

Branch McCracken's Indiana teams won the NCAA national title in 1940 and 1953, with the '53 team earning the nickname "the Hurryin' Hoosiers."

Knight in public and Robert Knight in private.

"I think that is exactly the way he wants it," says Powless. "I would give him a call and I would say there is a young man here I would like you to meet. And so we would go down to the pregame shoot-around at 10 o'clock in the morning and the first thing he says is, 'Why aren't you in class?' He wanted to know about that kid's life."

Knight succeeded, claims Powless, because of how he prepared. He demanded the most out of his players. He demanded that they knew where they were on the basketball court and why. He demanded that they go to school. He demanded that they properly represented the university. Not everyone could handle the demands.

When colleges recruited high school basketball star Isiah Thomas, Thomas' mother insisted he attend Indiana.

"Knight was the only coach guaranteeing Isiah would get an education. His mother liked what she heard and Isaiah became a Hoosier," explains Powless.

Thomas led Indiana to a national championship in 1981 as a sophomore and then left the school for a 13-year NBA career with the Detroit Pistons.

ADOLPH RUPP

"Coach Rupp was very, very kind to me," recalls Powless.

Adolph Rupp coached Kentucky basketball from 1930 to 1972. His teams won 876 games, four national championships and 27 conference championships. He also participated in one of college basketball's landmark events.

In 1966, Kentucky faced Texas-Western (now the University of Texas–El Paso) in the national championship game. The players did not really need uniforms. Texas-Western started five black players and Kentucky did not have a black player on their team. This contrast made news. At the time, many southern schools wouldn't even play a team with black players, let alone recruit one for their own team.

Rupp's Kentucky teams played teams with black players, but for most of his coaching career, Rupp either did not or could not recruit blacks to play at Kentucky. Even if Rupp wanted a black player, it would be a tough sell to ask an 18-year-old to come to a place where he would be subjected to racial slurs, threats on his life and rejection from just about everyone on campus.

It had some similarities to the recruiting problem Powless faced at Wisconsin, where he had to convince a prospect and his parents that Madison was a safe place for their young man despite the tear gas and protests they read about in the newspaper.

Rupp recruited against racism. Whether he himself was a racist may be debated until the Internet goes dark. But

Adolph "the Baron" Rupp

near the end of his career, he recruited Thomas Payne, a seven-foot-plus black player from Louisville.

Adolph "The Baron" Rupp first met John Powless when Powless starred at Flora High School. While Rupp wanted Powless to play for him, Powless chose Michigan and later transferred to Murray State.

Rupp could set his watch by the drills his Kentucky teams ran, whether he was at the practice or not.

"He could be sitting here with you and he would look at his watch and say, 'Well, they are doing three on three man weave right now.' And he would sit a little bit longer and you would say, 'Well, what are they doing now, Coach?' He would say they are doing the splits right now. They are doing it from the side. Or they are doing the points from the high post. He could tell you exactly what his team was doing, whether he was in the gym or not. It's part of what made him the great coach he was."

Powless and Rupp continued their relationship when Powless entered coaching, sharing film and comments of common opponents. Speaking to and with other coaches is part of what makes good coaches better.

"McGuire, Knight, Rupp and others were never beyond asking someone outside their own program for help," says Powless. "They were always looking for one more edge. That is why they were great."

Another common attribute Powless believes good coaches share is pressure. A coach is a celebrity on campus and beyond. But Powless believes the real pressure is on the athlete, not the coach.

"You expect the fan to have an opinion," he says. "You expect fans to call you and write you letters. And don't be offended. Everybody says there is great pressure. No, there is not pressure. The pressure is on the kids."

Powless remains friends with his fellow coaches and will still offer his thoughts to anyone who seeks him out. He does not like that his coach at Cincinnati, Ed Jucker, is not in the National Collegiate Basketball Hall of Fame.

"The first two years of his head coaching career he won the NCAA championship and the third year he took Cincinnati to the championship game again," says Powless. "And that bothers me. We tried to be Oscar Robertson without Oscar and that got us three losses in less than seven days. And we said we've got to change, but the season was on. We stayed up late, but we did it and Ed was our leader. It was nothing short of a miracle."

John Powless will always be a coach with or without a team.

"That internal part of you never leaves," he says. "I love the practices. I love the game, the kids, all of them."

Once a coach, always a coach: John with two "campers" at his annual tennis camp in Beaver Dam, Wisconsin.

Chapter 13

JPTC
JOHN POWLESS TENNIS CENTER

NBA teams pursued Powless to scout college players. Coaching tempted him, but something else started to occupy more and more of his time.

Madison businessmen John Fox and PGA member Dennis Tiziani built a golf course surrounded by condominiums and homes in a neighborhood known as Cherokee Marsh on the north side of Madison. The two approached Powless to see if he would be interested in building and running a tennis club to complement the property. He was interested, and he took them up on the offer. Three years later, Powless broke with Fox and Tiziani and started the John Powless Tennis Center on the city's west side—a facility that survives in the same spot today.

"I was still involved in tennis because kids I had as juniors eventually became Davis Cup players," says Powless. "I started getting calls to come play, which was really strange because I was grossly overweight. I would get called to play not only in this country, but abroad as well.

There wasn't enough money to sustain open, professional tennis then. Now they make more losing in the first round event than we made by winning those tournaments. But I was involved to a certain degree, and then there were times when I was asked to come and speak. That is where basketball and tennis were still combined in my life. But then tennis became a little more full-time. And then I got back into trying to play. But I was still so far out of shape. And it wasn't a matter of lung capacity. It was more my legs couldn't carry the additional weight. I was 70-some pounds more than I am now. Half of it went away right away. The other half stuck around for the ride."

In his heart, Powless knew he had coached his last basketball game in 1976. He still rooted for the Badgers, but his successor, Bill Cofield, let it be known that the former coach would not be welcome in the UW Field House. After another regime change, new coach Steve Yoder invited Powless to come and take a look at the team. It's what most coaches do in this somewhat exclusive fraternity.

"I liked being around it. It sort of brought the coaching back. It satisfied me to the point that I was doing a lot of things except coach. It still bothered me when Wisconsin didn't win, but it wasn't the end of the world like it was.

You are likely to see more than one Powless generation at The John Powless Tennis Center. That's John's son, Jason, stringing a racquet and Jason's son, Joe, working on his lob.

John's first son John D. Powless II (second from left) poses with his wife Helen, daughter Heidi, sons Taylor and Cord at Heidi's graduation from the University of Kentucky. Today the Powless' live in Olney, Illinois not too far from Flora.

Chapter 14

LIVE ON TV

College basketball and television are made for each other. The games last two hours and have plenty of commercial time for TV stations to sell. And college basketball delivers a coveted demographic to prime-time advertisers: men.

Yet despite this seemingly perfect match, some college athletic administrators in the 1980s still feared that broadcasting their games on TV would reduce the numbers of ticket buyers. Wisconsin already struggled to get fans to the Field House. A building that could hold eight thousand basketball fans usually hosted no more than five thousand. The so-called "Faithful Five Thousand" had plenty of room. Why would anyone watch a team on television when they wouldn't come to see them live?

The Faithful Five Thousand must have sensed something. Wisconsin started to win a few games, and by 1989 the Steve Yoder–led Badgers received an invitation to play in the National Invitational Tournament. While not as prestigious as the NCAA Tournament, it was at least the postseason—the first time the Badgers had played in a postseason game since 1947.

The NIT bid excited the success-starved Badger basketball fans, and a Madison TV station asked Powless to be part of the broadcast team. Two years later, the NIT invited the Badgers back, and the games were back on television, this time with John Powless as the "color commentator," dressed in his red madras-plaid pants and blue blazer.

Not only did the NIT invitations pique interest in Badger basketball, the ratings the games received pleased local TV executives. They rivaled the network offerings, and the local station could keep more of the ad revenue than they would have received from regular network programming.

In 1992, WMTV, the Madison NBC affiliate, launched a schedule of regular-season Badger games and hired Powless to cohost the broadcasts with WMTV sports director and anchor Mike Heller, who did the play-by-play. And, to the surprise of the doubters, attendance at the Field House increased.

Powless prepared almost as vigorously to broadcast games as he had to coach them. He often knew what play a team would run before they ran it. It wasn't exactly something the Big Ten didn't want Powless sharing with the viewers, but in his mind he was coaching the viewers.

No one knew the Wisconsin Badger basketball team better than Powless—so much so that when his friend and former rival Al Maguire came to Madison to cover the games for CBS, the first person he called was John Powless. Broadcasting Badger basketball put Powless back in the game.

In the 1992 season, Indiana had just crushed Wisconsin at Assembly Hall in Bloomington. As Powless and Heller were leaving the arena, a man and a boy approached Powless.

"Coach," said the man. "How have you been?"

Powless became engrossed in conversation with the pair as Heller, waiting nearby, checked his watch repeatedly, worried that he and Powless would miss their flight back to Madison.

Finally reunited, Heller asked Powless who the man was. Former player? Fellow coach? Long-lost cousin?

"I have no idea," Powless said.

Chapter 15

MR. SENIOR TENNIS

For Powless, the tennis bug eventually became impossible to shake, and it wasn't enough to run the John Powless Tennis Center in Madison, Wisconsin. Since he'd been old enough to stick out his thumb at the junction of U.S. Highways 50 and 45 in Flora, Powless simply had to play tennis. Something loosely called "senior tennis" gave him a chance to compete at the highest levels in his age group all over the world.

The International Tennis Federation (ITF) runs and coordinates tennis for virtually every age category. The ITF began with an idea from an early-20th-century tennis player and lawyer named Charles Duane Williams. He suggested an organization that would govern the growing sport of tennis. Tragically, Williams went down with the Titanic, but his idea lived on. In 1913, 12 tennis associations from around the world formed the International Lawn Tennis Federation. Not only does the ITF (as mentioned previously, they eventually dropped "lawn" from the name) rank players competing for Grand Slam titles, it runs

a healthy senior program that makes room for players up to 100 years old.

The senior tennis movement began after World War II. During the war, many soldiers played tennis on their leaves, often with their British counterparts. After the war ended, a group of veterans organized a few tournaments to keep up their skills and competitive spirits. An informal group of both British and American vets arranged to hold a tournament in Lake Placid, New York. They played for the Gordon Blair Cup.

"The Gordon Cup is still played the last weekend of July," says Powless. "These days we play in Canada one year and the U.S. the next. We play 45 matches over a three-day period and the winning country takes home the Gordon Cup. The Gordon Cup is the second-oldest cup in tennis after the Davis Cup."

While the ITF took senior tennis seriously, the United States Tennis Association considered the Gordon Cup a social event.

"We then recruited some of the top players in the game: Vic Seixas, Bobby Riggs, Gardnar Mulloy and others," says Powless. "It did get the USTA's attention, but we still did not get any support from them."

As this almost-informal senior tennis movement grew, so did the age categories. Powless and others went on to found Super Senior Tennis, which now includes a division for players age 95 and older. Recently, more than 30 players entered what's known as the "95s."

"We have every kind of tennis event you can imagine," says Powless. "Husband and wife mixed, father and son, mother and son, mother and daughter, grandfather and granddaughter—you name it and there's an event for you, no

Palm Springs Life

California's Prestige Magazine

APRIL 1993

PALM DESERT WELCOMES
10TH ANNUAL
PHOENIX CHALLENGE/
LOVE 50

Original Senior
Recreational
Interclub
Competition

matter how old you are."

And now there's even financial support from the USTA. Katrina Adams, the organization's current president, appointed volunteer committees, each with the charge of growing the sport of tennis.

"The Adult Competition Committee is one of them," says Powless. "I think the future of senior tennis is bright."

It was the ITF that first started sanctioning senior tournaments. The ITF organizes the categories for men and women by age in increments of five years. If you're between 35 and 40, you play in the "35s." If you're between 60 and 65 you play in the "60s," and so on.

Remembers Powless: "I just went to the 35s because these guys invited me to come down and play, because I had won the U.S. Southern Open, which has names of Jack Kramer and all the great players that had won the tournaments on the trophy. It was a big prestige thing to win this. You are a former player and they

Wimbledon Windmill Championships (left to right): K.J. Hippenstiel, Alex Kim, John, Peter Bronson and Larry Turville.

invite you to play, and you are going to get beat in the first or second round."

The United States and Canadian teams pose for a Gordon Cup photo.
John is seated in the second row near the American flag.

Except Powless didn't go home after the first or second round. Increasingly, he left these tournaments with world titles in both singles and doubles. And he was not even playing in his age group.

"I would go to Houston and play in the national 35s even though I was 45," says Powless. In 1996, Powless tore his Achilles tendon. Three operations over a five-year period kept him out of competitive tennis—or, for that matter, tennis on two feet.

"Probably my best tournament was when it was the National 55 and I had the Achilles injury and hadn't played a tournament point in five years," he says. "I was invited to speak at the event and I asked if there was an opening to play. The tournament director said yes, but it was in the 45s. My age put me in the 55s, but I had to get back to playing. So I went in to play and I was at least 12 years older than the rest of the 45s. I won without losing a set. I beat the number one ranked player in the world."

John Powless had returned to tennis.

"I couldn't run. I couldn't stand to wear a shoe. I had to cut out the back of a tennis shoe just to be out on the courts to teach. I had a sports chair, which is for wheelchair tennis, and I would wheel around and hit tennis balls in this wheelchair. I even went to the tennis camp and hit balls with the kids in a wheelchair. It's a very humbling experience.

"I hadn't played a tournament in five years and I was in Philadelphia to speak at a dinner. They had three age categories: 45, 50 and 55. I was 64 and I asked about playing, because my Achilles had finally healed so I could hit balls on two feet and run. They found a spot for me in the 55s, and I went out and won it. That was my return after the Achilles."

With the exception of the Grand Slam events—Wimbledon, the Australian Open, the French Open and the U.S. Open, competitive tennis grew as invitation-only events. Event organizers would send out invitations, attempting to land enough top players who might draw crowds large enough to at least cover the organizers' expenses.

(Left to right) Len Saputo, Jim Parker, John, Steve Wilkinson and Keith Dipram the USA team that won a world title in Montevideo, Uraguay.

"If the tournament hosts thought you would last until the final eight players, you might have received a plane ticket to and from the event, $35 a day for room and board and maybe a $150 appearance fee. Many would stay in private homes and pocket the per diem. But if you were one of the four they wanted in the semifinals, that number could double. A finalist might earn $1,500.

"Rod Laver told me he made $30,000 in eight months playing around the world. That was big money. A college coaching job was $6,000 a year at that time.

"Top players could travel from event to event, maybe pocketing a few dollars a day. These same top players picked their matches carefully, and some would be out of the tournament by the end of Thursday and headed for a more lucrative event on the weekend.

"Big parties, great fun and you make some money. I won't say you made a lot of it, but you had spending money. There were 300 guys trying to qualify for 32 open spots. So you would have 300 guys fighting, cheating, throwing racquets. The guys that didn't qualify didn't make any money. The 32 guys who did qualify were playing for a total of $10,000.

"Out of this haphazard way of recruiting players for a tournament grew a movement among players to move the money from under

John poses with the Gordon Cup with Canadian captain Vic Jansen and Monte Ganger.

the table to the top of the table. Only the top players and organizers were making any money; some of the players tanked early matches to play more lucrative private exhibitions a few days later. So the United States Tennis Association had to sanction open tennis events.

"We wanted them to put the money on top of the table and let us play for it. Gene Scott was a friend, and we approached USTA president Jim Dickey and suggested there was an audience for this. Whether that was the first step to get it done, I don't know, but we planted a seed."

Others tried to organize players. A union called the Association of Tennis Professionals (ATP) sprung up with Jack Kramer—the world's number-one player—as its first president. In 1974, ATP boycotted Wimbledon in a dispute with ITF, and 13 of the top 16 men's seeds boycotted the world's greatest tennis event.

Tennis—at least in the United States—struggled. The USTA did what they could with the money they had.

"In some respects the U.S. was broke," Powless says. "The best the U.S. could do was win enough early Davis Cup matches to get in a playoff against Australia in Australia and cash a check for $50,000. But they made a mistake one year and they won."

Winning meant hosting the next Davis Cup in America.

"That is when the USTA was broke, and that is when Billy Talbert and I say, 'You've got to start charging an entry fee,'" says Powless. "And if you want to host a tournament you have to pay a sanction fee for it. Otherwise we are finished. Tennis is over with. So that is how membership fees started for the

USTA."

While the international senior tennis movement allows players of any age to continue friendships, it is first and foremost competitive.

"They are out to win," says Powless. "They want to win every point.

"I was in Montreal with Allan Stone. Three hundred players tried to qualify for 16 spots. There was $10,000 in prize money. Because of the number of players trying to qualify, the tournament ran 24 hours a day. Allan Stone and I were doubles partners playing a night match against a team from Quebec. The line judge called a ball out against the Canadians. They were so upset, they approached the line judge and started shaking his chair. The judge jumped out of the chair and left. We were left alone to call our own lines and Stone said, 'No more questions. A call is a call. No bad calls.'

"So our opponents proceeded to make a series of bad calls, and Stone summoned them to the net. One of the guys was smirking and laughing, and Stone walked up to him and pop—punched him in the nose. The guy went down and didn't get up and Stone said, 'Play is continuous. The guy can't play. Our match. We're in the finals, John,' and we walked off. No one said a word."

While the senior tennis crowd remains competitive, a punch in the nose is a rare occurrence. The senior circuit is a very social movement as well.

John with United States Senior Davis Cup members Keith Dipram (left) and Adrian Bey.

"For a lot of people it may be the one thing they have left in life," says Powless. "They may have lost their mate of a lifetime, and the only other people they have are their fellow tennis players. While it's changed somewhat in the United States, outside the U.S. if a player loses his or her first match on Friday morning, they stick around the tournament until the finals on Sunday. There are social activities every night. They have formal awards ceremonies where you're standing on a podium like it's the Olympics.

"Senior tennis keeps you mentally and physically keen. It can extend your life. I watched a 97-year-old play a 93-year-old. When the match was over the 97-year-old said, 'I got to stop playing with these kids.' "

Forbes magazine wrote: "There's no better advisor on how to play masterful tennis after you've irretrievably lost that half step than John Powless, a.k.a. Mr. Senior Tennis."

Gordon Cup win in Lake Placid, New York. Ben Malaga, Bren Mackin, David Garry, Monte Ganger and John.

The 1998 official program of the USTA featured his photo on page 15 and called him "the high priest of senior tennis."

"There are many sports of a lifetime, but when it comes to tennis it is the most beneficial, physically, mentally and socially," says Powless. "I don't hear from basketball players very often. But I hear from a tennis player somewhere around the world every day of my life."

By 2005, he also heard from his knees. He was 73 years old with a lot of mileage on his body.

"I had gone almost a year where I couldn't run," Powless says. "We had the knees scoped two or three times and it just didn't work. And so it became obvious it was time for the replacement. I had my shoulder done twice—most recently in 2011.

"With the knees it's just as important what you do before the surgery as after the surgery, maybe more so. You need to condition the legs with weights to increase muscle memory—so it comes back quicker than if you don't do it. Dr. Rick Glad told me that you'll get your life back to normal, but the tennis is questionable. I told him there's only one reason I'm doing it and that's to get back playing tennis. At the time the companies that made the knee replacement did not want to hear about someone coming back and being competitive in a sport. Within three months I played the U.S. Championships and won."

Powless would once again summon his competitive spirit. This time, though, he threw all of it at rehabilitation. If there was a record for knee replacement recuperation, Powless would own that trophy, too.

"I was told by Dr. Glad that the exterior part—the feeling in the knee—would take almost 12 months, and it was almost 12 months to the day when I started to get all the feeling back in my knee," says Powless. "There were other things that I did, but all of it was pretty aggressive. The rehab people were great. What I wanted to do was to get back to playing tennis. So, I created my own rehabilitation program so that I could do it from my house and my neighbor's pool."

He would often work 10 hours a day: lifting weights, riding bikes and running in his neighbor's pool. He did two hour-long pool workouts a day, in March, in Wisconsin, with a water temperature of 42 degrees.

"I took my tennis racquet with me," he says. "The resistance of the water against my legs was beneficial. I would take one step and emulate a volley. I went one step, then two, then three and eventually four steps. I did it with ground strokes. I did it with overhead motion. I did it with serve and motion. I would sprint across the pool. I had an upright and a recumbent bike. That was more difficult in making the complete loop with the pedal. I could only do a half a turn and the pain

John with doubles partner Lenny Lindborg with the first place trophy at the Senior World Championships in Osaka, Japan.

John rehabs his new knees in his neighbor's pool in March, 2007.

was so bad I thought I was going to croak. But I made it and soon it didn't feel so bad. Really, what you're doing is getting your knee and your body to accept each other.

"One day I was bored and I wanted to get out of the house. I woke up at three in the morning and I went through some routines and I decided I was going to go to the tennis club and try to hit a few balls against the wall. It took me an hour to get into the car. The garage door was open and I was in the car and I thought I'd better see if I could get out of the car. I couldn't get out. I had my cell phone but I had to wait until my son Jason woke up and went to the tennis club so I could get the hell out of the car. So it was three in the morning when I decided to go to the club. It was four in the morning by the time I got in the car. And I sat in the car until six in the morning before I could call Jason to come and help me out of the car. So that's when Jason said we're going to have to drive around and find something that I can get in and out of. It was less than three weeks after the surgery."

It was not the first time Powless recovered quickly from a physcial setback. More than sixty years ago doctors told him he would never play tennis again after breaking his neck in college. He was back on the court within six months.

THE HOSTAGE

John Powless has seen the world playing senior tennis. He relishes most of his experiences. But in the late 1980s he found himself playing on the island of Brac in the Adriatic Sea. Brac is part of Croatia, but then it was still part of Yugoslavia, a country put together by Nazi Germany in World War II. Croatia, Serbia and Bosnia became Yugoslavia. Powless and his Senior Davis Cup teammates landed behind the Iron Curtain in a country dominated by the Soviet Union. At the time, the Soviet stronghold was weakening. In a few short years, the Berlin Wall would come down, the

Soviet Union would dissolve and the Iron Curtain would fall. Yugoslavia was splitting apart. Tensions among opposing factions, the Serbs, the Bosnians and the Croatians, were rising, and the team was advised to stay close together on and off the court.

"It came time to fly out and everyone else on the team was on to the next tournament, but I had a stress fracture so I had to come back to Madison to get it treated," says Powless. "I got to the airport. I got to the gate and there was nothing there. I got to another gate where there were a lot of people and I was having trouble making my way to the agent, when suddenly all the people left. They weren't flying anywhere. They were just at the airport and gone. So I finally talked to the agent and he said, 'We'll fly to Belgrade and you can fly to Chicago from there.' So I flew to Belgrade and a woman who looked like a mean villain in a bad spy movie told me I can't board the plane to Chicago. She told me I had to leave. I told her I'm not leaving. I'm staying here.

"All of a sudden these two guys with shoulder weapons came up to me. Meanwhile, I saw a guy in the back with a younger woman. He started yelling, and the guys with guns took the butts of their weapons and beat him on top of his head and the blood came gushing out.

In Antalya, Turkey at the ITF World Championships (left to right): Jack Vedervelt, George McCabe and Saul Snyder.

In Sydney, Australia with Jim Osborne, Jim Parker, Charley Hoevel-
erer, Monte Ganger, David Nash and John.

They grabbed him by the ankles and dragged him away.

"Finally the two guys with the guns came back and took me outside to a bus. There was a driver. One guy with a gun went to the back of the bus. The other guy went to the front of the bus and I was the only other person on the bus. They took me downtown and checked me into a hotel, never saying a word. The room was tiny, with paper-thin walls. I looked out the window and saw the first McDonald's behind the Iron Curtain and I thought, at least I can get a Big Mac. I went down to the lobby, opened the door and there was a tank with the barrel of the gun pointing right at me. So now I thought, I'll just eat at the hotel.

"All this time I kept asking questions and they kept claiming they couldn't understand me, which I knew they could.

"I stayed at that hotel for three days. Finally, the same bus, same two guys, same driver came and picked me up and took me to the airport. I boarded a Yugo Airlines plane and came home. To this day I have no idea why they kept me in that hotel."

SOUTH AFRICA

While playing in Sun City, South Africa, Powless decided to take a side trip into the Pilanesberg National Park. In 1979, the South African government fenced in seven thousand acres to protect wildlife from poachers and reintroduce native species to the area. It remains a success and attracts tourists from all over the world.

In the park, you can drive among the wildlife, and if you're a bit more adventurous, walk among the wildlife. Guides roam the park to let people know when and where they should be in or out of their cars.

"We drove up and saw an elephant stomping on a dropped tree, trying to get nourishment from it," says Powless. "I was standing about 20 feet away taking pictures. A ranger came by and told me he thought I'd taken enough pictures. I took a few more and he said, 'No, stop and leave because if you irritate him he will not only trash your car, he'll roll it down the hill for you.'

"At the same time we heard gunfire. This ranger rushed up to us and told us to get back in our car. Apparently, according to the ranger, there were hundreds and hundreds of lions waiting to eat lunch. After that it was just scary.

"It was getting dark and time to leave, and we saw what looked like fireflies in front of the car. The fireflies were the eyes of a string of female lions. They approached the car, passed the car in a single line followed by the king himself. He marked the car to let us know this was his territory.

"They had a cookout for us in the bush, and two of the people who prepared the cookout had a little extra sauce and wandered away from the cookout. They were never seen again."

AUSTRALIA

When he travels to places like Australia, Powless travels alone—all six-foot-six of him. Before he leaves Madison, he arranges everything for the trip: practice times, entry fees, accommodations. He prepares by drinking only water to insure that he stays hydrated once he hits land. He flies from Madison to Los Angeles and then endures the 18-hour trek from L.A. to Melbourne.

Once he hits the ground, it takes four to five days to let his body adapt to the time change and the warm climate.

In 2012, he landed on the heels of a storm, with temperatures in the lower 50s. During his first match four days later, the temperature rose to 102 degrees,

John with former British Davis Cup player Gus Holden and tennis writer Mark Winters at Roland-Garros in Paris..

and that would be the coolest—if it can be cool at 102—day of the tournament. Not only did he face his opponents, he battled the oppressive heat any way he could. He froze his hats in ice water. They were dry as a bone 15 minutes later.

After reaching the round of eight, Powless faced Keith Edwards of Australia, an opponent he had never played before. He lost the first game and the first two points of the second game.

"I thought, I've just flown halfway around the world and this guy is going to beat me and I'll have to turn around and go back home tomorrow," says Powless. But he told himself to stick to his game plan and not do any more or any less. After all, it is a strategy that has worked for Powless for 70 years. The match turned. Powless won in two sets.

Next it was on to the semifinals to face Adrian Alle of Australia, the second-ranked player in the world in this age group. Powless won in two sets without losing a game.

In the finals, he faced Lorne Maine, an opponent he's faced a dozen or more times in his lifetime and the top-ranked player in his age group in the world. Yet Powless has beaten him every time they've played. Still, if there was any betting, the money wasn't on Powless.

"It got a little irritating, because people were saying, 'I really hope you can at least give him a good match because no one's been able to do that,'" says Powless. "I wanted to bite my tongue in half because I wasn't telling anyone I had never lost to the guy."

The match was set. Both players warmed up in the hundred-plus-degree heat, when a storm rolled in, drenching the courts. The storm rolled out just as quickly as it rolled in. Now, there was not a cloud in the sky, but the players had to play in the 30-miles-per-hour winds that chased the storm. Powless served first.

"I couldn't see the ball," he says. "When I threw it up to serve, it went right in the sun. Even when I threw it above the sun, it came right back down in the sun. I was serving blind."

Powless tried to adjust his toss, but that only threw off his serve, and he lost the first game. But Maine had the same trouble when he served on that side of the court, and the two went back and forth, battling each other and the sun. Powless won the first set, and more of the same transpired in the second set, until Powless found himself serving to win the match and Mother Nature intervened one more time. This time it was a small, lonely cloud.

"I could see the ball on my toss for the first time. So I hit the first serve in a normal situation for the first time in more than two hours of tennis."

Powless saw the ball and won the title. And he won the way he always has: He prepares for everything possible, from stocking up on water to stay hydrated to keeping a ready supply of Band-Aids in case he gets a cut to knowing how his opponent plays. It's what he admires in all the great coaches and players he's known.

"It's all preparation," says Powless.

But even with all the preparation, there are still times when things do not go as planned on the tennis court.

"The one thing all great tennis players do when that happens is to keep constant eye contact with the ball," he says. "I visually burn a hole in the ball. It's impossible to see a small spot on the ball, but you have to convince yourself you can. Watch the ball as it hits the surface. Make sure your racquet is ready to hit that ball as soon as it hits the surface. You keep the ball in front of you; otherwise the ball will control you.

"When a ball doesn't go in and you know you hit it well, all you can do is forget it. If you get upset you'll expended too much negative energy.

"There are two rooms. One of them has very few people. Those are the people who handle the pressure. The other room is packed. Those are the people waiting to get into it. You have to find a way within you to overcome the times when things are not going your way. There are people you play against that you've made them hit 50 cross-court backhands. All of a sudden you get impatient and hit it down the line and you lose the point. Some people just don't want to stick with what's working."

John's 2000 induction to the USTA/Midwest Section Hall of Fame with son, Jason, daughter-in-law Laura Jeanne, and grandson Joe.

THE LAST MATCH

Jean Borotra played with the famous Four Musketeers, a team of French Davis Cup players that dominated the sport in the 1920s and 1930s. He was known for his lavish parties after a victory (he won 19 Grand Slam titles) and his snappy berets. One writer called him "the cocky guy with the racy blue beret." He was the heart and soul of the French team that won six David Cups in a row. He survived a Nazi concentration camp, where he spent six months in solitary confinement. He played his last doubles match with John at age 94 at Rolan-Garros..

Chapter 16

PRESIDENTS & PRINCES

GEORGE H.W. BUSH

Tennis opened many doors for Powless. When then–vice president George H.W. Bush needed a doubles partner, he asked Powless. Their opponents were two wealthy potential contributors to Bush's upcoming presidential campaign. Bush and Powless won the first set without losing a game. They won the first five games of the next set, when Powless took his partner aside.

"I said, 'George, don't you think we ought to let these guys win at least one game? You do want them to contribute, don't you?'

"Bush said, 'Screw them, I can't help it if they can't play.' I said, 'What about the money?' He said, 'They're either going to give me the money or not, whether they win a game or not.'"

Powless would later hold a tennis clinic on the White House tennis courts after his playing partner became the 41st president of the United States.

"DAVY CROCKETT"

Actor Fess Parker was another doubles partner. Powless and Parker met when Parker was filming a movie called *Davy Crockett and the River Pirates* from 1956.

Walt Disney had just picked Parker to play the legendary American hero Davy Crockett, and the River Pirates movie marked one of his first appearances as the character. Powless appeared as an extra and spent most of his time on-screen letting Parker or co-star Buddy Ebsen throw him in the river.

The *Davy Crockett: King of the Wild Frontier* TV series made Fess Parker an American icon. Despite Davy Crockett's relatively short run as a television series, American kids became smitten with all things Crockett, including the character's coonskin cap. After struggling to shake the Crockett stereotype as an actor, Parker become TV's *Daniel Boone* in the 1960s, in which he played virtually the same character, only with a different name. When that popular show ended after six years, Parker found he couldn't shake the characters he'd played, so he left acting and went on to a successful career as a vintner and southern California real estate developer.

And he loved tennis. Powless and Parker renewed their acquaintance at a tennis event called the Rafael Osuna Cup in Mexico a few years later and played as a doubles team.

John with White House assistant chief of staff Michael Deaver and actor Fess Parker.

"The biggest thing is that he loved to play. He said to me, 'I don't travel, but if there's tennis involved, I'll be there.' He was a competitive player. He played college football in Texas and he was a big, strong guy. We'd put him in one spot and if he could put a racquet on it, chances were he'd put it away."

The Parker-Powless doubles team won the Osuna Cup one year, and the two remained close friends until Parker died in 2010.

"He never backed away from the public. He was nice to everybody. He was the same guy that he was in the movies."

TENNIS AT THE WHITE HOUSE

Through his friendship with Fess Parker, Powless was invited to participate in an exhibition at the White House. Parker and Ronald Reagan were friends from their days in Hollywood. First Lady Nancy Reagan's cause was the so-called war on drugs, and the exhibition was organized to raise money to support her efforts.

Left to right: Veronica Hamel, Fess Parker and his wife Marcy, John's wife Sheree Powless and John.

"We walked in and out of the White House in our tennis clothes with racquets," says Powless. "Nancy walked up to us and said, 'My boyfriend and I are going to have cocktails and dinner and we'd like you to join us,' so pretty soon we were having drinks with the president of the United States.

"Once Nancy Reagan asked, 'Who's that big kid over there?' The big kid was Michael Jordan. Everybody was there. Tom Selleck came up to us and said, 'Mr. Parker, you probably don't remember me, but when I was a kid you gave us a tour of the studio.' Fess said, 'Oh I remember that.' That's how classy a guy Fess Parker was. Tom turned to me and said, 'Mr. Powless, you probably don't remember me either, but you sent me a questionnaire to fill out when I was a high school basketball player in southern California.' "

Selleck would play for the University of Southern California instead of Wisconsin and then become "Magnum P.I." on television.

"Fess and I had just finished hitting balls and President Reagan came by the locker room for a visit. So there I am—a kid from Flora, Illinois—drinking a Coors with the president of the United States and Davy Crockett."

"The Reagans were such down-to-earth people," remembers Powless. "They treated us great."

THE EMPEROR'S COURT

President Jerry Ford was looking for a college bas-ketball team to go on a goodwill tour of Japan. Ford and Powless' former boss, UW athletic director Ivan Williamson, had been friends at Yale. Through this connection, the president invited the Badgers.

"The president said there are places in Japan where they've never seen Westerners and that's where we'd like you to go. We would practice and thousands of schoolkids came to see us. They didn't peep a word. It was a great experience for our players."

Near the end of the trip, Powless found himself on the top floor of the Nippon Steel Company, which overlooked the Imperial Palace compound of Japan's Emperor Hirohito. He noticed a clay tennis court, still his favorite surface to play on.

"I told my hosts I'd sure like to play there," he says. "They had no idea I played tennis, but after I told them I played with the likes of Rod Laver and others, I found myself across the net from the future emperor of Japan, Akihito. I still get an invitation to his birthday party every year, although I've never gone.

"We stayed in touch and when he came to Chicago, they drove him up to Madison to play at the club. They sent se-curity ahead of time. They told me where we could be on the court. They told me to stand back when he arrived. He'll talk to you. You don't talk to him. That's not my personality, so when he walked in I walked up and shook hands with him. So we started hitting balls and he finally said, 'When are you going to start talking to me and coaching me?' I told him they told me I couldn't talk to him.

"So I started helping him, and when I grabbed his arm to show him where a better racquet position was, the entire security delegation rushed the court with their samurais drawn. They didn't really have swords, but you get the idea. But after everyone calmed down I helped him with his game, and he left Madison a better tennis player.

"It's too bad the rest of the world couldn't witness this. We're all here together. The tennis ball doesn't care who you are. The basketball doesn't care what color you are."

PRINCE BERNHARD

Powless almost started another international incident in the Netherlands in 1991 during the Jubieumboek (jubilee) celebrating the 60th anniversary of the International Lawn Tennis Club of the Netherlands. Prince Bernhard, the host of the event, loved tennis and sat courtside and watched as the best senior tennis teams in the world competed for the Windmill Cup.

Powless spotted Prince Bernhard sitting alone. Powless knew the prince liked to fly planes and drink whiskey with their mutual friend, world-famous test pilot Chuck Yeager, so he went over to say hello. Dutch security immediately descended on the conversation. The prince quickly dismissed the security, and Powless and Prince Bernhard continued their conversation.

At one point Powless noticed that the prince, sitting courtside in the baking sun, had no hat, so he offered him one, while softly chiding him about exposing himself to the sun without protection.

The two remained friends until the prince died in 2004 at age 93.

These international senior tennis tournaments are part competition and part social events with lavish parties, dinners and sightseeing. John Pow-

less' U.S. team took second in the 1991 tournament, losing to the Netherlands in the finals.

After the prince handed out the trophies and medals, Powless surprised the prince with a Prince tennis racquet with the prominent Prince logo painted on the strings.

"Just hold this up when you need a taxi," Powless told the prince, getting a big laugh from the surrounding entourage. He also promised to send a Prince tennis bag to Prince Bernhard—"If I can have your address," said Powless.

By all accounts, Prince Bernhard enjoyed life.

"I saw him moving slowly once and he told me he cracked his ribs when he slipped as he was getting into an airplane for a joy ride with Yeager," says Powless. "He said he and Yeager drank a little too much whiskey the night before."

What almost nobody knows is that the prince also enjoyed collecting Powless' tennis warm-ups. And only the prince knows why, but somewhere in the House of Orange was a closet with used tennis sweats.

"I never understood why," says Powless. "They didn't fit him, that's for sure."

SANTA CLAUS AND PRINCESS DI

As Powless travels to tennis tournaments around the world, he brings along tennis ball key chains and lanyards to pass out the to pilots and crew members of the airlines. One trip in the early 1990s had him traveling to London in December. After passing out his gifts, he was approached by a crew member.

"You're kind of like Santa Claus," Powless remembers the crew member saying.

The crew asked Powless to stay in London an extra day and play the part of Santa at a fund-raiser the airlines held every year for orphans.

"I'd love to be Santa Claus," he told them.

At the fund-raising event, crew members dressed like elves, and one woman played the part of Mrs. Claus.

"She was plump," remembers Powless. "We went up and passed out goodies to all these children, and I was trying like mad not to cry, but my eyes were full of tears. The kids were so excited. They had real reindeer and the whole thing.

"Afterward they had a cocktail reception for us and I caught the glance of an attractive woman. I looked again and she said, 'Yes, I am.'"

It was Princess Diana.

Powless asked her why she was there.

"Why, Santa, I'm Mrs. Claus," she told him.

Chapter 17

THE ABCs

"You really win tournaments in between tournaments or in the off-season," says the wise and seasoned Powless. "In basketball you want the player who's just as good if not better in practice than in the game.

"In tennis, 80 percent of the points won on the planet are over after your opponent hits it twice.

"My advice to coaches is to simplify the game. If you make it complicated for your players, you'll lose more players than you keep. It's the A-B-Cs, the 1-2-3s. If you have good racquet preparation, no matter what your body is doing, you have a good chance to get the ball back. Body position is number two, but when it comes time to hit the ball, that's finished. Too many people take too big of a swing or have too much body movement. And third is to let your hands bring the racquet through the ball and your body will follow. It's the wrist to the end of your fingers and your ankles to the end of your toes. The rest of it is along for the ride. So just simplify it.

"Most people don't want to sacrifice enough to let it be simple. You've got to say to yourself, 'I just love punishing myself mentally and physi-

cally.' There is no substitute for experience. You have to experience the failure as well as the success. Some people will say, 'That was a lucky shot.' They don't realize that you hit thousands and thousands of balls to make that lucky shot.

"Sometimes you catch yourself walking back to serve match point and you say, 'I've forgotten how to serve.' You step back for a moment and you instantly give yourself an instructional moment. One time, Roger Federer was asked why he stepped back for a moment before serving for the match. The reporter asked him if he was thinking about what he would say in his acceptance speech, and he said that he was teaching himself how to serve. Everyone laughed, but he said, 'No, that's exactly what I was doing.' It was nice to hear the top player in the game confirm all the anguish I had gone through over the years.

"It's not the years you've spent doing something. It's the hours and minutes you've spent doing something that make you good at it.

"You have to spend time on your deficiencies. But you need to spend the same amount of time on what you do well or you'll lose your ability to do those things well. If you don't hit your backhand, find a way to get it in until you can hit your forehand. It puts a lot of pressure on your opponent trying to find your backhand.

"If you want to get better at something, don't pick multiple points to work on. Pick one. Pick one of the points that is vital to your success. It doesn't matter what the sport. It's what you do when the ball is in the air to prepare yourself to make the play. For example, tell yourself that today I'm going to watch the ball. Today when the ball is coming out of the ball machine I'm going to make sure that the racquet is back. It's motionless. It's not moving when I'm moving. When the ball arrives, I'll stroke it.

"You have to visualize what you're going to do on the court before you get to the court. You have to visualize winning points, losing points, having a bad day, having a good day.

"You have to get out of town every once in a while. There are a lot of so-called experts who never leave town because they fear not being successful. I marvel at everyone with ability to do things well because I admire the time they've spent working on them."

HITTING BALLS AGAINST THE WALL

John Powless still loves to coach and play tennis, whether working with his Sweet Swingers at his tennis club or helping the U.S. senior team win the Mulloy Cup in Europe.

"You just coach them to death and they love it," he says. "Coaching never leaves you. I hurt inside when the Badgers lose a basketball game, and I think every year is going to be exciting. That's what gives you life every year."

While he's passionate about coaching and helping others be successful on the court, Powless reserves part of every day for John Powless. Whether it's playing with his son, Jason, or against a wall like he did at Murray State, Powless rarely lets a day go by without hitting tennis balls.

"That's my fix. It's the way you feel after you finish," he says.

It's 1991, and though he's the center of attention at an event at the All England Lawn Tennis and Croquet Club in Wimbledon, England, no one is talking to John Powless. He's standing alone at center court of Wimbledon, crying. He's just been made a member of the International Club of the All England Lawn Tennis and Croquet Club. It is tennis mecca. Standing in the empty stadium where the greatest players have sealed their reputations, John Powless can reflect on what tennis, and sports, mean to him. The USTA calls tennis "a game for life."

They need look no further for a poster boy than John Powless.

PHOTO CREDITS

University of Wisconsin: 66-74, 76-77, 79-80
Indiana University Archives, 88-89
University of Kentucky Special Collections Research Center: 91
Murray State University: 28, 30-35, 37-38, 44
Marquette University: 86
Illinois Digital Archives, Illinois Secretary of State: vii
Shutterstock: 123
Dan Smith: 92-94, 120, 124, 127, 129
Angelina Marquez Smith: vi, viii, 129-131
The Powless Family: 1-24, 29,39, 51, 53, 55-56, 58-59, 65, 75, 78, 81-84, 95-96, 98, 99-111, 113, 116-119
Library of Congress: 26
Florida State University: 41-42
German Federal Archive: 114
KNLBT, NLTennis: 115, 121-122
University of Cincinnati: 45-50, 60, 62-63
University of Iowa: 85
Jeffery Pohorski: 125

ACKNOWLEDGEMENTS

John and Dan would like to thank our friends and family who helped bring this book to you.

Angelina Smith for reading and commenting on the manuscript maybe a thousand times.

Brenna Nardi for editing the manuscript.

Barbara Walsh for editing and proofing the manuscript.

The Powless family for taking and sharing many wonderful photos in the book.

All the friends we've known through our careers in athletics and media and everyone who paid a little attention to what we've done.

Dan Smith is an Emmy award-winning writer and producer with more than 30 hours of network television credits including programs for the Discovery Channel, National Geographic Channels International and others. He also contributes to Madison Magazine. This is his first book.